Urban Anthropology

ELEMENTS OF ANTHROPOLOGY
A Series of Introductions

Urban Anthropology

J. Douglas Uzzell
Rice University

Ronald Provencher
Northern Illinois University

wcb

WM. C. BROWN COMPANY PUBLISHERS
Dubuque, Iowa

ANTHROPOLOGY SERIES

Consulting Editors
Frank Johnston
University of Pennsylvania

Henry Selby
Temple University

Contents

Preface

Urban Anthropology introduces the field it names. The first part deals with basic concepts and with prehistoric and historical studies of the development and nature of urban places around the world. The second part is a discussion of the theoretical and methodological issues raised by the recent beginning of ethnographic studies in contemporary urban places. Questions discussed in *Urban Anthropology* include a consideration of what anthropology offers that sociology does not and what methodological changes, if any, anthropologists must make in their studies of contemporary urban places. The book is both substantive and theoretical. It is also argumentative. Though designed primarily as an introductory textbook, it discusses issues that are unresolved and that are of interest to all anthropologists who do urban studies.

We made arbitrary decisions in the design of this book, from settling on a title to deciding how to treat contemporary studies. The present title, though decently short, does not emphasize enough our belief that anthropological studies of urban places should closely resemble anthropological studies of nonurban places. Another title, "The Anthropological Study of Complex Societies, Focusing on Urban Places," reflected our belief more accurately, but seemed unnecessarily cumbersome. We fell back on

the present title for the sake of simplicity and hoped that our readers would not tire before reaching our final statement in defense of this point.

We were very concerned to bring together archaeological and ethnological studies of urban places, because both are "urban anthropology," and because our ability to combine and learn from the two is one of the strengths of the discipline of anthropology. The first three chapters deal with basic concepts and models of urban evolution, and the last four deal with studies in and of contemporary places. Because the theoretical issues are less obtrusive and the substantive information less controversial in the former than in the latter, the first three chapters seem more substantive and less contentious than the last four.

Throughout the book we have asked many questions and provided few answers because that best reflects the state of the art. We begin by questioning the usual definitions of basic concepts and of the place of anthropology in social science. In chapter 2, we examine some of the common explanations for the evolution of urban societies. And in chapter 3, we doubt the validity of a common "progressive" typology of cities even while describing that typology. In chapters 4 and 5, we consider the fitness of anthropology for urban studies—primarily in contrast with sociology. In chapter 6, we sample recently conducted studies. And in chapter 7, we suggest directions for future studies.

Repeatedly, we give sociology a hard critique. In so doing, we have in mind the brand of sociology that C. Wright Mills has called "abstracted empiricism." For the record, we are aware that there are many "good guys" among sociologists, and we even cite some of them in the book.

The book is argumentative, and we expect and invite counter argument from those who do not share our philosophical views. We have very specific ideas about what urban studies should be. We have not attempted to give equal representation to positions in conflict with our own, feeling that those positions are over represented in the literature. Scientifically, we are unawed by the precedent of eighteenth- and nineteenth-century physical science, and we feel that repeated attempts by social scientists to use the paradigms of classical physics have had an effect that is analogous to that of a baseball team trying to use hockey equipment.

Throughout, our approach has been rough-and-tumble. We are exuberant but easygoing. We seek to engage you.

J.D.U.
R.P.

1 | Is Urban Anthropology Necessary?

THE IMPORTANCE OF URBAN STUDIES

Because most of us live in cities today, we tend to forget that urban living for the vast majority of the world's peoples is very recent. Even in the United States most people at the turn of the century lived in rural areas. Nowadays more and more of us are born in cities, work in cities, and buy and sell goods that are made and marketed in cities. We talk about "fleeing the city" when we move to the suburbs, but the suburbs are urban places, too. By moving to the suburbs we are not slowing the growth of urbanism. We are merely a part of its spread. And those of use who live in the country are dependent as never before on urban markets and products and urban-centered systems of transportation and communication.

Our most urgent problems are related to the rapid growth of urban environments, which has gone along with economic development and population growth. And to understand those problems, we have to understand how cities become cities; and how people meet their daily needs, satisfy their basic wants or values, and adapt to the urban environment. All too often urban planning has proceeded without that understanding, with the result that even the best intentioned programs have fallen short of their expectations.

Competent urban researchers cannot, should not, provide quick and easy answers to urban problems. Too often "applied research" that is intended to provide solutions to current problems caters entirely to the demands of the moment, supplying data that support proposals put forward by political forces, without regard to long-term effects. Planning strategies that do not include substantial budgets emphasizing pure research are nearsighted and ineffective, because pure research is needed to identify the general roots of a problem rather than specify a cure for some perceived ill. What would we think of a doctor who prescribed pills for every symptom the patient listed, and neglected to think about the disease that was causing the symptoms? Yet, too often this is what our urban planners do. Caseworkers to bring down gang warfare, food stamps to eliminate hunger, more police to bring down crime, neighborhood-action programs to get the houses painted and the garbage picked up. Pills for symptoms that have political sex appeal! Obviously, urban studies are more important today than ever.

Urban studies have always been important to anthropologists. Even while we have focused most of our research on villages and mobile tribes and bands, our goal has always been to understand all human life. *Where* we have studied has shaped our research techniques. And admittedly, methods developed for studying small populations are sometimes difficult to use with large populations.

But we do not want to throw away our methods. We have always been better than other social scientists at describing and understanding the contexts of peoples' lives. We understand that a lot of the supposedly crazy things that people do are not crazy at all, if we will take the time to understand their culture and their way of perceiving a situation. So, although we complain about our own methodology, we prefer it to the methodologies of urban sociologists and geographers who are not so well endowed with techniques for gaining insight into the rich detail of everyday life in cities. What we are trying to do is grasp the whole picture, complex as it is, at the same time that we plumb the intricacies of peoples' daily lives, choices, motives, and problems. If that ideal is unattainable, it nevertheless points us in the right direction.

THE CONCEPT OF URBANISM

We Westerners have mixed feelings about cities and about urbanism. We think of cities as being places where exciting things happen, but also as sinks of sin and oppression. We romantically long for the countryside, which we idealize. Mind you, people who live in the countryside, or people who were peasants or tribesmen before cities were invented, do not (and did not) seem to share these feelings. The romance of the rural atmosphere was created by poets who lived in cities and wrote about shepherds and shepherdesses for other city dwellers.

The feeling that somehow the countryside is a better place to live has turned up in social science theorizing. Emile Durkheim,[1] for example, felt that rural societies were self-sufficient: every family could grow its own food, make its own clothes and technological equipment, and, in that sense, operate as an autonomous unit. Society was made up of similar units: households or kinship groups that could function on their own. But the city bred the division of labor. Every family became dependent on the production and labor of others, and so complex did this organization become that many of those groups on which one depended were neither kin, nor friend, nor even acquaintance. A contract had to be created between the different units to ensure that each family got the necessities of life. The shoemaker made shoes for families that needed them, while the farmer produced food for the shoemaker. It was as though each type of producer were a different bodily organ, and society was the organism itself. It depended on the efficient working of each organ carrying out its specific task, but could only exist if they all functioned in their proper way. Supposedly, complex social machines are more apt to break down (become "diseased" or "morally corrupt") than simple ones because their many and varied parts mesh in many different ways and are thereby more interdependent (i.e. less "dependable"). Durkheim changed his opinion on this matter as he became more familiar as a research worker with urban social organization. But only a very few nineteenth-century scholars, such as Adna Weber, contested the general Western viewpoint that urban society is morally corrupt.[2] Most, like Josiah Strong, echoed a favorite theme of the "romantic" philosophers—that modern urbanism produces moral degenera-

---

1. E. Durkheim, *The Division of Labour in Society* (Glencoe: Free Press, 1947—first published 1893); E. Durkheim, *The Elementary Forms of the Religious Life, a Study of Religious Sociology,* trans. J. W. Swain (Glencoe: Free Press, 1947—first published in 1912).

2. A. F. Weber, *Growth of Cities in the Nineteenth Century* (New York: Macmillan Co., 1899).

tion.[3] Nineteenth-century scholars described their cities as places where materialistic values overwhelmed traditional spiritual and moral values; where traditional family structure degenerated, natural reproductive increase was insufficient to perpetuate the population, and city-born citizens comprised the largest proportion of the lowest social classes (which, of course, were viewed as including the largest proportion of criminals and degenerates). During the first three-quarters of the twentieth century this basic Western assumption of the immorality of urban life did not become less popular.

Reformers and philosophers—Jane Addams, Georg Simmel, Oswald Spengler, Louis Wirth, John Galbraith, Lewis Mumford, Edward Banfield, Charles Reich, and hundreds of others—have continued to produce works that are based on the assumption that city life has a degenerate effect on intimate social groups and that such groups are the only natural contexts within which normal (i.e., "moral") personalities can develop and thrive.[4] Supposedly, city dwellers are released from social controls that are based on the total personal knowledge of other members of their intimate groups, and interactions become superficial, transitory, and specialized, allowing individuals greater freedom to exploit each other. An individual need not be a consistent personality from one context to another. He can be as many persons as there are different audiences for his performances. Schizoid personalities (which, of course, are "abnormal") are said to result from these circumstances.[5]

Many superficially objective conceptions of urbanism, although not in themselves moralistic, are based on this notion of urban social organization and its unfavorable comparison to rural social organization. Tönnies described the contrast in terms of *gemeinschaft* and *gesellschaft*.[6] Gemein-schaft relationships are closely knit, kin based, and strongly local; gesellschaft relationships are impersonal, economically and politically based, and strongly territorial. The first is supposed to be typical of rural and the second typical of urban communities. Discussions of the contrast between status and contract relationships (Maine), societas and civitas (Morgan), traditional and rational (Weber), and the folk-urban continuum (Redfield) make essentially the same point.[7] In each instance, urbanism is defined according to the nature of social relationships, allowing one to conceive of urbanism without cities, although the original authors of these conceptions did not reveal this possibility.

3. J. Strong, *The Twentieth Century City* (New York: Baker and Taylor, 1898).

4. J. Addams, *The Spirit of Youth* (New York: Macmillan Co., 1909); G. Simmel, "Metropolis and Mental Life," in *The Sociology of Georg Simmel*, trans. K. Wolff (Glencoe: Free Press, 1950); O. Spengler, *The Decline of the West* (New York: Alfred A. Knopf, 1928); L. Wirth, "Urbanism as a Way of Life," *American Journal of Sociology* 44 (1938):1-24; J. K. Galbraith, *The New Industrial State* (Boston: Houghton Mifflin Co., 1967); E. C. Banfield, *The Unheavenly City* (Boston: Little, Brown & Co., 1970); C. A. Reich, *The Greening of America* (New York: Random House, 1970); L. Mumford, *The City in History: Its Origins, Its Transformations, and Its Prospects* (New York: Harcourt Brace Jovanovich, 1961).

5. Wirth, "Urbanism as a Way of Life."

6. F. Tonnies, *Community and Society*, trans. C. P. Loomis (East Lansing: Michigan State University Press, 1957).

7. H.J.S. Maine, *Ancient Law Its Connection with the Early History of Society and Its Relation to Modern Ideas* (London: Oxford University Press, 1931—first published 1861); L. H. Morgan, *Ancient Society, or, Researches in the Lines of Human Progress from Savagery through Barbarism to Civilization* (New York: Charles H. Kerr, 1877); M. Weber, *The Theory of Social and Economic Organization*, trans. A. M. Henderson and T. Parsons (New York: Oxford University Press, 1947), pp. 136-138; R. Redfield, *The Primitive World and its Transformations* (Ithaca: Cornell University Press, 1953).

Most definitions are not of "urbanism" but of "a city," or "an urban place." Trait lists with an emphasis on demographic characteristics are a common approach. Total population is the most ubiquitous measure in legal definitions of urbanism, but standards vary from country to country. In the United States census, the minimum total population of an urban place is twenty-five hundred. There are higher and lower standards of minimum total population. Scholars interested in cross-national comparisons usually set the minimal size of urban places arbitrarily at fifty thousand or one hundred thousand. Lower standards, such as that of the United States census, would in other countries include many villages whose occupants are peasant fishermen or peasant farmers. Population density is another measure of urbanism, but the same problem arises. Some fishing villages and agricultural areas of the non-Western world have higher population densities than some urban communities of the West. Other demographic measures that could be employed include heterogeneity (according to ethnic identity, occupation, or social class), geographic and social mobility, and age and sex disproportions.[8] Size and density are used most often to define urban places, probably because of their simplicity rather than for any more cogent reason.

Perhaps the most useful definition of a city is that of Horace Miner. He says that a city is a center of dominance.[9] Such dominance may be religious, political, military, commercial, or industrial (singly or in combination). The idea that cities are centers of dominance is fine as far as describing the role of cities is concerned, but it does not take us very far. A modern version of the same theory, developed by Friedmann,[10] which emphasizes the increased productive efficiency that is brought about by getting people and ideas (information) in close proximity, has the same fault. It is true, but it doesn't take you very far.

There are other related ways of thinking about the city. "Central place theory" was developed in geography and provides ways of thinking about the optimum location for urban centers. It enables us to ask whether the city is located effectively so as to best communicate with its hinterland (the countryside it serves) by way of redistributing services, goods, and information. When it can be determined that the location is suboptimal—that is, not the best—we can begin to look into the reasons why. Similarly the notion of "over-urbanization" takes the same idea, but emphasizes that the process of urbanization can get out of hand and lower the efficiency of the city as a processor of goods and information. Discussions of "primate cities"—that is, cities that are far bigger than neighboring cities and completely dominate the other cities as well as the rural environment—is part of the same line of thinking. Such thinking envisions cities as becoming so gargantuan as to absorb the countryside, leaving a desert beyond its borders. As you can see, urban theorists have focused on the role of cities as centers of redistribution; as market places for ideas, goods and people; as centers where communication between the shoemaker, the farmer, the artisan, and the priest is facilitated so as to enable society to function like an organism.[11]

8. *See*, for example, J. C. Mitchell, "Theoretical Orientations in African Urban Studies," in *The Social Anthropology of Complex Societies*, A.S.A. Monographs 4, ed. M. Banton (London: Tavistock Publications, 1966), pp. 48-51.

9. H. M. Miner, ed., *The City in Modern Africa* (New York: Praeger Publishers, 1967), pp. 5-10.

10. J. Friedmann, "An Information Model of Urbanization," *Urban Affairs Quarterly* 4(1968): 235-44.

11. B. J. L. Berry and A. Pred, *Central Place Studies; a Bibliography of Theory and Applications* (Philadelphia: Regional Science Research Institute, 1961); N. V. Sovani, "The Analysis of 'Over-Urbanization'," *Economic Development and Cultural*

THE CONCEPT OF URBANIZATION

Experts define urbanization no more precisely nor consistently than they define urbanism. Generally, urbanization is conceived of as a process that produces or increases urban characteristics of a population. It has been defined as an increase in the proportion of city dwellers in a population; an absorption of tribal and peasant peoples into a modern state; a change to an impersonal style in social relationships; and an increase in the range of alternatives for individuals in most aspects of life.[12]

A much more ambitious definition of urbanization is implied by Reissman's "typology of urbanization."[13] He combines four indices—urbanism (proportion of city dwellers), industrialism (proportion of industrial contribution to total production), development of the middle class (per capita income), and nationalism (literacy rate)—to arrange nations on a scale from least to most urbanized. The result is supposed to illustrate the transition from preindustrial to industrial urbanism. Reissman's typology deserves criticism on several counts so far as its logic is concerned. But more important to us is that once again it does not help very much. Even though he uses data from non-Western society, he judges the degree of urbanization by Western standards. And what we need is a way of thinking about urbanization that is not biased, but general.

The same problems turn up in the discussion of "over-urbanization."

Over-urbanization occurs, we are told, when a high ratio of urban to rural population in a country is not matched by a high ratio of nonagricultural workers to agricultural workers. The "normal" relationship between these two ratios is supposed to be like that in the West. Social scientists who have been concerned with over-urbanization are in the intellectual position of assuming that urbanization in the West has not been "over-" or "under-" done, but "just right," and they

have also assumed that the West is at least one evolutionary stage ahead of other cultures.

Anthropologists rarely have dealt with urbanism or urbanization on such a grand scale, although there are examples of anthropological studies of urban regions, cities, and towns.[14] In the past, urban anthropologists have tended to specialize in small communities and single institutions within urban contexts, studying enclaves of ethnic minorities, immigrants from rural

Change 12(1964):113-22; A. S. Linsky, "Some Generalizations Concerning Primate Cities." *Annals of the American Academy of Geographers* 55 (1965):506-13; R. Redfield and M. B. Singer, "The Cultural Role of Cities," *Economic Development and Cultural Change* 3(1954):53-73; M. Weber, *The City,* trans. D. Martindale and G. Neuwirth (Glencoe: The Free Press, 1958); J. A. Quinn, "The Burgess Zonal Hypothesis and Its Critics," *American Sociological Review* 5(1940): 210-18; A. Southall, "The Density of Role-Relationships as a Universal Index of Urbanization," in *Urban Anthropology; Cross-Cultural Studies of Urbanization,* ed. A. Southall (New York: Oxford University Press, 1973); M. Banton, "Urbanization and Role Analysis," in Southall, *Urban Anthropology;* V. G. Childe, "The Urban Revolution," *Town Planning Review* 21(1950):3-17.

12. K. Davis et al., "Urbanization and the Development of Pre-Industrial Areas," *Economic Development and Cultural Change* 3(1954):6-24; A. Southall, "Introduction," in Southall, *Urban Anthropology;* O. Lewis, *La Vida* (New York: Random House, 1965).

13. L. Reissman, *The Urban Process: Cities in Industrial Societies* (Glencoe: The Free Press, 1964).

14. *See,* for example, P. J. Pelto, "Research Strategies in the Study of Complex Societies: The Ciudad-Industrial Project," in *The Anthropology of Urban Environments,* Society for Applied Anthropology Monograph Number 11, ed. T. Weaver and D. White (Boulder: The Society for Applied Anthropology, 1972); H. Miner, *The Primitive City of Timbucktoo* (Princeton: Princeton University Press, 1953); A. Gallaher, *Plainville Fifteen Years Later* (New York: Columbia University Press, 1961).

areas, occupational groups, religious institutions, and markets. Perhaps their most prolific topic has been rural-urban migration. One reason for this dominance of migration studies in the literature of urban anthropology is that rural migration is a worldwide phenomenon that has accompanied the Industrial Revolution and has gained great momentum in the past thirty years; and anthropologists have better theories, methods, and training for studying it than other social scientists. When considering the meaning of urbanization, most anthropologists probably think first of the many anthropological studies of rural-urban migration and of the effects of urban environment and culture on the culture of rural migrants.

We almost touched upon another important meaning of urbanization earlier when noting the Western bias against urban life and the way this bias has affected Western conceptions of urbanism. We noted that social behavioral definitions of urbanism suggest that urbanism may occur outside the context of cities. Urbanization without cities is possible, too, depending on our definitions. Urbanization may be seen as a change to patterns of behavior that are like those associated with life in modern cities. Urbanization of this sort became common outside the territories of cities in the twentieth century as a result of revolutions in the technology of communication and transportation and in the organization of commerce and nationalism.

Because these cultural revolutions have been associated with the recent spread of Western European influence, a spread of unparalleled extent and impact in the history of human society, there is a sense in which urbanization, modernization, and Westernization are equivalent terms. We of the West can hardly avoid our thoughtless ethnocentric equation of these terms. We too often forget that non-Western societies, producers of raw materials and consumers of manufactured goods, have had as much part in the Industrial Revolution as we. The Industrial Revolution has transformed their societies just as it has transformed our own. And their societies are as modern as ours in this sense. Trapped by our ethnocentrism, we view as modernization and urbanization only those changes which are manifestations of Western influence. This ethnocentrism distorts the theoretical and methodological bases of the social sciences that have dealt primarily with Western European and Anglo-American societies. One of the primary values of anthropological theory and method is that it has been tested by the fires of intensive research in non-Western societies. Western ethnocentrism remains, undoubtedly, but it is under control and it clouds the vision of anthropologists much less frequently than that of other social scientists.

ANTHROPOLOGY AND THE STUDY OF URBAN PLACES

A kind of "Just So Story" has become current for explaining why anthropologists have recently intensified their study of urban places.[15] With minor variations, the story begins with our running out of tribal groups to study in the 1930s and turning to the study of peasants, who were still plentiful. Then, after World War II, when tribesmen and peasants began moving in large numbers to towns and cities, we followed them.

15. *See,* for example, W. Mangin, "Introduction," in *Peasants in Cities: Readings in the Anthropology of Urbanization,* ed. W. Mangin (Boston: Houghton Mifflin Co., 1970), A Southall, "Introduction," in Southall, *Urban Anthropology;* G. M. Foster and R. V. Kemper, "Introduction," in *Anthropologists in Cities,* ed. G. M. Foster and R. V. Kemper (Boston: Little, Brown & Co., 1974). By "Just So Story," we do not mean that the story is entirely fictional or that the story is comparable in quality to stories of Rudyard Kipling. We mean only that the story is overly facile.

This story is dangerously misleading. Its most subversive effect is to support the popular but false notion that social/cultural anthropology is essentially a discipline with rural interests and that in the study of urban places anthropologists are unlettered newcomers, poaching on the preserve of sociologists and urban geographers. The truth, as Leonard Plotnicov has pointed out, is that

. . . from the time of Tylor to the present, anthropologists have always protested . . . that our framework of observation and discourse includes all known examples of human society and culture, and that our comparative approach has as its ultimate purpose the scientific understanding of *all* human social institutions and cultures.[16] (italics in the original)

Research is not anthropological because of the place in which it is carried out; but rather, it is anthropological because of the way it is done, and because of the kind of knowledge it produces—because of the special perspectives of anthropology. Anthropologists are specially trained to record and compare folk theories of social experience. Ordinarily, they must live a year or more as participants in a foreign society before being recognized as professionals. During that time they conduct research for their doctoral dissertations, but the experience itself is a very important part of anthropological training. It habituates them to patterns of logic, values, social behavior, and artifacts that differ from those of their own culture. When they return to the cultural context of their own society, they see from a new perspective and notice patterns of logic, values, behaviors, and artifacts that they previously took for granted. Long-term participant observation in a foreign culture has helped them to learn different techniques of looking and has helped prepare their minds for different ways of seeing. Having once learned a different way of seeing and knowing, their minds are opened to more rapid

learning of different lifeways and to clearer perception of their own lifeways. In this sense, extensive experience of anthropologists in rural and non-Western societies gives them special qualification for studying urban and Western societies. In effect, anthropologists are specialists at forming hypotheses about the ways in which human social and mental life is organized.

We have insisted that anthropology is not confined to rural and non-Western societies. We also insist that urban anthropology is concerned with urban societies and cultures of all times and places. If we were to skip lightly over other examples of urbanism in a rush to focus on contemporary urbanism in our own culture, we would lose the special perspective of anthropology that derives from careful comparison. Without that perspective, urban problems cannot be identified properly, much less solved.

For Further Reading

Abu-Lughad, J. "The City is Dead—Long Live the City: Some Thoughts on Urbanism," in *Urbanism in World Perspective, a Reader.* Edited by S. F. Fava. New York: Thomas Y. Crowell Co., 1968. About our ambivalent attitude toward cities.

Gulick, J. "Urban Anthropology: Its Present and Future," in *New York Academy of Sciences,* ser. 2, vol. 25, 1962. The classic initial definition of the field.

Plotnicov, L. "Anthropological Fieldwork in Modern and Local Urban Context," in *Urban Anthropology* 2(2) (1973):248-64. The best explanation to date of the need for urban anthropology.

Scientific American, September 1965. Special issue on cities.

Wheatley, P. "The Concept of Urbanism," in *Man, Settlement and Urbanism.* Edited by

16. L. Plotnicov, "Anthropological Fieldwork in Modern and Local Contexts," in *Urban Anthropology* 2(2)(Fall 1973):250.

P. J. Ucko, R. Tringham, and G. W. Dimbleby. London: Duckworth, 1972. The most scholarly discussion of the concept of urbanism and perhaps the longest footnote on the concept of urbanization.

Bibliography

Durkheim, E. 1947—first published 1893. *The Division of Labour in Society*. Glencoe: Free Press.

Maine, H. J. S. 1931—first published 1861. *Ancient Law Its Connection with the Early History of Society and Its Relation to Modern Ideas*. London: Oxford University Press.

Tonnies, F. 1957. *Community and Society*. Translated by C. P. Loomis. East Lansing: Michigan State University Press.

Weber, A. F. 1899. *Growth of Cities in the Nineteenth Century*. New York: Macmillan, Co.

Wirth, L. 1938. "Urbanism as a Way of Life." *American Journal of Sociology* 44:1-24.

2 | Theories of Origin and Development

INTRODUCTION

The origins of states and of urbanism are intertwined. Theories that explain one usually help to explain the other because urban centers are a common characteristic of states. Most theories of origin and development are concerned with the question—"What are the circumstances usually associated with increases of size and complexity of societies?"

Before going on we need to comment upon the usage of four words—*scale, size, density,* and *complexity.* In everyday language, as well as in social science jargon, one of the meanings of *scale* is *size.* When we say that something is large, that is a statement about the scale or size of the object. We need not say that it is "large size" or that it is "large scale," but only that it is "large." *Density* refers to the number of objects in a particular space. Ordinarily we use density as a measure of the number of individuals per unit of land. But we extend its meaning metaphorically in the term "role density." Role density is high where, on the average, people have many identities or roles (e.g., kinsman, boss, creditor) vis-à-vis other people. For more than a century, social scientists have been suggesting that the size and density of a population together affect the pattern of relationships among members of the population. One of the ways

relationships are affected is that the larger and more dense the population, the fewer the number of roles one person plays vis-à-vis another and the more relationships are specialized. That is, role density varies inversely with population size and density. Because it is awkward to keep writing "population size and density," we will use "scale" instead. *Complexity* of a society refers to stratification and specialization. A society is more complex if there are more social strata, more specialization of labor, and a more complex exchange of goods and services. Similarly, other things being equal, a society is more complex if more cultural traditions are present.

Increases of scale initially precede increases of complexity. That is, increased food supply allows increases in population density, or increased population density forces development of new sources of food, and one or the other of these processes results in an increase of complexity. Secondarily, an increase of complexity may result in an increase in the scale of a society. As this "circle of causation" continues, access to goods, services, information and power becomes increasingly difficult because there are more people, and everyone depends on others to a much greater degree. The creation of an information clearing house, or storage center, becomes necessary. One simply cannot sustain one's self in a complex world, if one does not know where the resources, skills, power and influence, ideas and personnel are. Lacking computers, the most efficient kind of storage place is a town or village. People move together and exchange information, and store it in their memories. The general word for hamlets, villages, towns, and such is *nucleated settlement.*

Nucleated settlements are not necessarily cities. Villages and towns qualify as nucleated settlements, too. They are smaller and less complex forms of nucleation that preceded cities as the dominant forms of settlement when states were evolving and that succeeded cities when states were devolving. In fully developed states they function as first and second levels of nucleation in hierarchies of settlements dominated by cities.

BANDS, TRIBES, AND CHIEFDOMS

Even villages, the least of the nucleated forms of settlement, are recent phenomena that first appeared after several million years of human social life. During most of their first million years of experience, human beings were food collectors. They hunted, dug roots, picked fruits and leaves, gathered grass seeds, collected mollusks and insects, and fished, according to the natural availability of food sources and the naturally and culturally molded dictates of appetite. Except in areas where abundant food supplies were available throughout the year, food collectors lived in simply organized, small-scale societies—bands of no more than fifty persons.[1]

These bands did not live in permanent settlements. They moved their camps whenever necessary to find new sources of food and water. Sometimes they changed the size and composition of their groups in order to take better advantage of food resources. When food resources were scattered, bands broke up into smaller groups. When food resources were concentrated in a few areas, bands joined other bands. Sometimes small groups of men left the main camps and lived separately from the women and children in order to pursue big game animals more effectively. In other instances, small groups of women and children established temporary camps near sources of plant food. Relatively small amounts of energy were harnessed and consumed. The most skilled and experienced person in a particular activity led the group in that activity. Leadership was very informal and was based on persuasion and example. Statuses were differentiated only on the basis of sex and age and major residential group. Systems of knowledge were relatively unspecialized and accessible to all. Each group was an entity joined to others by shifting personnel and by fragile and ritualized relations of exchange. Marriage exchange was a primary basis of alliance between groups. Ties of marriage provided the basis for claims to the resources of another group almost as powerful as blood ties. Territorial claims of groups were not defined according to absolute boundaries, but rather according to core areas that contained major resources and according to rights of access to resources in other areas. There were neither explicit boundaries nor border guards.

Life was probably more complicated in areas that had rich supplies of food the year around. Of course, in the past, before they lost ground to or became food producers, food collectors inhabited such places. Where food was more plentiful it is very likely that population was more dense, local groups larger, levels of energy consumption higher, settlements more permanent, spe-

1. E. R. Service, *Primitive Social Organization: An Evolutionary Perspective* (New York: Random House, 1962); E. R. Service, *The Hunters* (Englewood Cliffs: Prentice-Hall, 1966).

cial statuses more numerous, knowledge more specialized and less accessible, leaders more powerful, relations between groups more comprehensive, and territories more carefully bounded. For example, the coastal areas of northern California, Oregon, Washington, and British Columbia supported relatively complex and large-scale societies of food collectors at the time Europeans first entered those areas; certain small areas in what is now the USSR supported very dense populations of more or less permanently settled big-game hunters during the Upper Palaeolithic (11,000 to 20,000 years ago); and the walled town of Jericho was founded more than eight thousand years ago in the Jordan river valley (more than a thousand years before agriculture was practiced in that area). In each of these instances a very large and dependable supply of protein was easily available because of immense populations of particular food species—salmon, elephant, and cereal grain.[2] Also in these instances, nucleated settlements were at sites that could control access to highly valued resources such as the best spots for placing fish weirs and traps, spots of easy ambush on established elephant trails, and an oasis in an otherwise dry land. Groups fortunate enough to have full claim to valuable resources not only regulated access of foreign groups but may have thus favored foreign groups differentially. Also, some individuals within the owning group may have had greater access to resources than others. The seeds of cultural and social heterogeneity would have been sown, and hereditary claims to special statuses (greater access) would have become more important. Although larger in scale and more complex than most societies based on food collecting, the societies in these examples were tribes or chiefdoms, at most. None was as complex and large as a state. Their nucleated settlements were mere villages or towns.

The Peruvian coast may offer prehistoric evidences of more or less sedentary villages of food collectors who eventually became food producers. At first their settled way of life was made possible by the richness of food sources in the immediate environment. Eventually they domesticated a few species of plants, but the first cultivated plants were industrial plants such as cotton and gourd rather than food plants. Later edible plants from the Andean highlands, the Amazon basin, and Central America arrived in the area and were cultivated. But new means to larger food supplies seem to have merely supported rather than initiated the development of nucleated settlement on the Peruvian coast.[3]

These examples illustrate that in favored circumstances a food-collecting economy can support societies that are large and complex enough to have small nucleated settlements. Also, they seem to indicate the importance of a large and dependable food supply for the development of complex societies. Domestication of food species usually increases their productivity and dependability. Economies based on domesticated rather than wild food species can support larger, more sedentary populations, and everyone agrees that the domestication of food species, the "food-producing revolution," (so-called because of the increased control over food sources), preceded the development of states and of cities. In other

2. E. E. Ruyle, "Slavery, Surplus, and Stratification on the Northwest Coast: The Ethnoenergetics of the Incipient Stratification System," *Current Anthropology* 14 (1973): 603-31; A. L. Mongait, *Archaeology in the U.S.S.R.* (Moscow: Foreign Languages Publishing House, 1959); K. M. Kenyon, *Digging Up Jericho: the Results of the Jericho Excavations, 1952-1956* (New York: Praeger Publishers, 1957).

3. T. C. Patterson, "The Emergence of Food Production in Central Peru," *Prehistoric Agriculture*, ed. S. Struever (Garden City: Natural History Press, 1971).

words, they view the "Urban Revolution" as an aftermath of the Food-Producing Revolution.

THE FOOD-PRODUCING REVOLUTION

The Food-Producing Revolution was a process that began whenever food collectors succeeded in attempts to stabilize and expand the ecological niches of plant and animal species that were major sources of food. This process occurred not once but many times and in many different areas of the world.[4] Different kinds of plants and animals were domesticated in different areas, and each area experienced a separate Food-Producing Revolution. Everywhere the process was slow, and in many instances it did not reach full fruition. In some instances, such as the irrigation of wild areas by the Owens Valley Paiutes in native North America and the replanting of pieces of wild tuber by the Yir Yiront, tribesmen of Australia, effective methods of controlling the ecological niches of food species were developed but did not lead to actual domestication of food species. Or domestication of food species was well developed early, as in Southeast Asia, Mexico, and the Amazon Basin, but did not lead quickly to development of states and urbanism.

Fire was probably one of the earliest and most common means employed by human beings to stabilize or extend the range of certain species artificially.[5] Living plants and seeds of different species differ in their reaction to fire. Some are completely destroyed, others are invigorated, and still others are only slightly affected. Because grasses are generally more resistant than trees to fire, hunters and herders of large grassland animals periodically set fire to bushlands and forests. They extend the area of grassland, thereby increasing the food supply of the grass-eating game animals and allowing their populations to increase, and thus increasing the food supply of human

hunters or herders. Slash-and-burn horticulture, in which fields are regularly burned off and planted, may be one of the oldest forms of the Food-Producing Revolution.

As population growth continued, year after year, food collectors were tempted more and more to increase the populations of food species. Their major technique for accomplishing this was to move food species to sources of water. These semi-domesticated food species changed rapidly, and some developed new qualities that enhanced their value as food plants. Most commonly, cultivated plants developed larger food parts and less effective mechanisms of seed dispersal. As food became more plentiful and less dispersed, people devoted more time to cultivation and less to collecting wild foods. This process of narrowing the range of food species required many centuries. Permanent villages developed in areas suitable for agriculture, but larger settlements and systems of settlements did not develop for thousands of years. Population increased gradually until about three thousand years ago, when irrigation systems provided new means of extending the area suitable for the cultivation of food plants. Even then, large nucleated settlements did not develop rapidly.

CEREAL GRAINS AND THE URBAN REVOLUTION

The most rapid development of large nucleated settlements occurred in the Tigris-Euphrates river valleys of Mesopotamia.[6]

4. L. R. Binford, "Post-Pleistocene Adaptations," in *New Perspectives in Archaeology*, ed. S. R. Binford and L. R. Binford (Chicago: Aldine Publishing Co., 1968).

5. H. T. Lewis, "The Role of Fire in the Domestication of Plants and Animals in Southwest Asia: A Hypothesis," *Man* 7(1972):195-222.

6. V. G. Childe, "The Urban Revolution," *Town Planning Review* 21(1950):3-17.

Truly urban life began there about five thousand years ago—the earliest anywhere. Even there it was not a sudden development. Food collectors had established permanent villages in the hilly flanks of the valley area (a zone extending from Palestine, Syria, and Cilicia across the piedmont zone of Turkey and northern Iraq to Iran, the Caspian shore and Turkestan, and also across the Agean in Macedonia) by about nine thousand years ago. In many areas they came to depend on wild barley and wheat as staple foods. These cereals occurred naturally and their seeds were thus easily gathered. Moreover, the seeds could be stored for a year or more, until the next harvest, and they could be transported over long distances without spoilage. Fairly large numbers of persons were required for the harvest because the grain shattered within a week or so of the time that it ripened. The whole crop had to be harvested within the span of several weeks. Naturally, those wild varieties that were least subject to shattering were favored by food collectors who rushed to harvest as much of the crop as they could before it fell to the ground. But within the span of several weeks, each group of harvesters could acquire enough grain to last a whole year. They had only to store it. The first permanent villages may have been as much for storage of grain as for habitation. Villages did not grow into larger nucleations in the hilly flanks area. Rather, barley and wheat growing diffused into the valleys where villages became towns, and towns became cities.[7]

The process of moving the cereal grains down into the valley area was at least as significant as the process of domestication. Insufficient rainfall in the valleys prevented the cereals from growing there naturally. Human beings cleared wild vegetation from areas next to the rivers and planted cereals there, where water was available. New selection pressures changed the cereals, and their utility as food species increased; and cereal growers became increasingly dependent on cereal grain as they abandoned other subsistence activities in favor of cultivating grain. The grain farmers were not alone in the valleys. Fishermen, hunters, gatherers, and horticulturalists all lived close to each other. But the avenue to increased density was through cereal agriculture, which could easily become the core of an integrated economy because it produced large food surpluses. The products of the fishermen and hunters were readily acquired by cereal agriculturists with their surpluses of grain, and because of this easy availability of grain, other subsistence technologies could become increasingly specialized and productive. Specialization simplified the technology of subsistence for individual groups, allowing each to do a single thing very well with great productivity, rather than doing many things more or less adequately with indifferent results.

Grain agriculture is commonly associated with the development of states and urbanism. The staple foods of urban civilizations were barley and wheat in Mesopotamia and Europe; wheat in Egypt and northwestern India and northern China; rice in southern China and Southeast Asia and Japan; and maize in the New World. Many lesser grains, such as kaoling in northern China, quinoa in Peru, and rye in northern Europe, can be added to this list. And we cannot but wonder why grains, more than, say, root crops, should be so commonly associated with the development of complex, large-scale societies. Manioc (tapioca) produces

7. R. J. Braidwood, "The Agricultural Revolution," *Scientific American* (Sept. 1960); K. V. Flannery, "Origins and Ecological Effects of Early Domestication in Iran and the Near East," in, *Man, Settlement and Urbanism,* ed. P. J. Ucko, R. Tringham, and G. W. Dimbeley (London: Duckworth, 1972); F. Hole and K. V. Flannery, "The Prehistory of Southwestern Iran: A Preliminary Report," *Proceedings of the Prehistory Society* 33 (1967):147-206.

more calories per unit of land than any grain, and other root crops such as potatoes, yams, and taro easily match the caloric production of grains.

The advantage of grains as staple foods of urbanizing societies is that they are more complete than roots as food. A population can subsist on grain alone for longer periods. Grains have more protein than root crops and they produce higher rates of fertility in human populations, thereby increasing density, which is an important dimension of the Urban Revolution. Also, grains are generally more productive per unit of labor, than root crops, and their requirements for labor occur in shorter spans of time, which (potentially) leaves a large labor force free to do the work of society for longer periods of time. Usually, the easiest way to increase production of cereal grains is to increase the amount of cultivated land. More often, the easiest way to increase production in root-crop horticulture is to increase labor rather than land. Possibly, this leads grain agriculturists to place a higher value on land and to have more elaborate conceptions of land ownership and use. Finally—and this returns to a point made in previous paragraphs—cereal grains are less amenable than root crops to mixed cultivation in which there is more variety of crops and less specialization of production.

Specialization is important to the development of organizational complexity and scale because of its implications for dependency and efficiency. In three instances, Southeast Asia, Mexico, and the Amazon Basin, the Food-Producing Revolution preceded the Urban Revolution by a very long period of time. Millennia separated these two "revolutions" in all three instances. In Southeast Asia, urban development did not begin until after wet rice agriculture began to supplant root and fruit crop horticulture about three thousand years ago. Urban development began in Mexico about the same

time, perhaps partially in response to a benchmark in the prolonged development of maize as a grain crop. In both instances we suspect that the specialized nature of grain agriculture was a key factor in the development of productive efficiency and economic dependency. Although large villages with populations up to two thousand developed along the Amazon and its tributaries, complex states never did develop.[8]

NUCLEATION: ECONOMIC INTEGRATION AND POLITICAL CENTRALIZATION

Specialization is not very productive unless an efficient mode of integrating the various specializations exists. At the beginning of the Urban Revolution in Mesopotamia, when villages were becoming towns, exchange of specialized products was coordinated by officials of the temples. These officials administered parish corporations that had mixed congregations of farmers, fishermen, herdsmen, and craftsmen. Parishioners contributed their specialized products to the temple for redistribution to other parishioners and were given credit so that they could draw other kinds of products from the temple warehouse. The earliest known examples of writing, more than five-thousand-years old, are accounts of these contributions. Other kinds of corporations, administered by wealthy individuals and military officials, developed along the same lines as parish corporations.

Priests did not rule Mesopotamian societies. In the beginning of the Urban Revolution, towns were ruled by councils. Such councils were composed of the elders of the several parishes of the town, and they ap-

8. D. Lathrap, *The Upper Amazon* (New York: Praeger, 1970); R. L. Carneiro, "The Transition from Hunting to Horticulture in the Amazon Basin," *Proceedings of the VIIIth International Congress of Anthropology and Ethnological Science* (Tokyo-Kyoto, 1968).

pointed other secular officials, such as temporary war leaders. As warfare became more common and war leaders became permanent officials, councils lost their political powers. War leaders became generals and kings.[9] Kings developed royal corporations whose wealth rivaled and eventually surpassed those of religious officials. Moreover, royal corporations included a greater variety of specialists than parish corporations—soldiers, entertainers, and long-distance traders, as well as religious specialists, craftsmen, farmers, herdsmen, and fishermen. Many of the specialists of royal corporations were not producers of food; they had truly urban occupations.

Members of corporations that were controlled by kings, generals, and other private persons may have been under more coercion than members of parish corporations to donate their surplus products and labor for the convenience and support of others. That is, their donations may have been demanded in the form of tribute, taxes, and corvée labor. Taxation would have been a very important means of directly stimulating the production of food surpluses by agriculturists, and corvée labor would have been an important means of developing capital resources, such as large-scale irrigation systems, that were beyond the capabilities of individuals or small groups.[10] Both were means of forcing the production of a surplus. Individuals had to meet their own ordinary subsistence needs and, in addition, produce food and labor for the maintenance of rulers and of specialists who did not produce food. Slavery, which was concomitant with the large-scale and incessant warfare that accompanied development of royal institutions, provided a surplus, too. Surpluses from slavery were derived not so much from the addition of persons as from the ease with which slaves could be compelled to labor beyond the bare requirements for their subsistence. The example of slaves probably was not lost on freemen who merely contributed taxes and occasional corvée labor.

Internal markets, as such, were never an important means of distributing the products of specialists in Mesopotamian societies. Temple storehouses, of course, had approximately the same distributive function as markets, and officials who supervised the distribution of various products might be likened to merchants. But the mode of distribution was very different from that of a free market. Donations of surplus goods were like tithes or taxes to the extent that they were not freely given but rather levied for the needs of other members of the corporation. Even long-distance trade was carefully controlled in Mesopotamia. Before the advent of kings, traders formed their own corporations and towns, and their contact with ordinary townspeople was mediated by officials of parish corporations. Later, they came under control of kings and were absorbed into royal corporations. The warehouses of long-distance traders were located near the gates of Mesopotamian cities or in separate towns. From the time of urban beginnings until after the time of Herodotus, in the fifth century B.C., Mesopotamian cities did not have market places.[11]

Urbanism developed almost as early in Egypt as in Mesopotamia. Probably Egyptian urbanism owed much to the Mesopotamian example, but it differed. From the earliest times, urban centers of Egypt were primarily the residences of royal officials. Egyptian royalty were also the highest of-

9. R. McC. Adams, *The Evolution of Urban Society: Early Mesopotamia and Prehispanic Mexico* (Chicago: Aldine Publishing Co., 1966).

10. E. R. Wolf, *Peasants* (Englewood Cliffs: Prentice-Hall, 1966).

11. K. Polanyi, C. M. Arensberg, and H. W. Pearson, eds., *Trade and Market in the Early Empires; Economies in History and Theory* (Glencoe: The Free Press, 1957).

ficials of the state, and it was their right to build new cities and relocate urban populations at will. They claimed surplus through tithes to temples, taxes, corvée labor, and slavery; and they redistributed it to non-food-producing specialists and through public works to ordinary citizens. Cities did not flourish in ancient Egypt. It came as close as any example to being a state without urbanism. Ethiopia is another such example.[12] Long-distance trade was important in ancient Egypt as a means of realizing greater wealth from grain surpluses and of acquiring scarce materials. Long-distance trade was controlled by the state. Local markets were not well developed.

Markets and trade played an important role in urban development in some other areas. East of Mesopotamia, between Mesopotamia and the Indus river valley, Elamite towns developed about as early as Mesopotamian towns. These towns had specialized economies which were based on abundant supplies of steatite in that area. Elamites quarried stone and traded it in bulk and as finished artifacts over long distances to Mesopotamia and India. They also traded in the products of other peoples, and were dependent on other peoples for supplies of food and other necessities. Trade was the lifeblood of Elamite society. It was much more important than redistribution as a means of organizing production.

Trade was equally important in the development of the Indus valley civilization. Long-distance trade with the easternmost Elamite towns, such as that evidenced by the remains at Tepe Yahya, was important, and local markets were well developed, too. Evidences from archaeological excavations at Harappa and Mahenjo Daro indicate that different kinds of occupations were well defined and that the practitioners of each occupation were members of a distinctive social grouping that occupied its own particular area of the city. Market places and the houses of merchants were prominent

architectural features of the urban scene. Palaces and temples may have existed, but they have not been identified among the ruins. The largest and most central architectural complexes of these early Indus valley towns were either public baths or central graneries—no one knows for certain. As in the case of Elamite towns, trade was one of the most important factors contributing to the development of urbanism.

Both trade and redistribution were important from the beginning of urbanism in Mexico. Archaeological evidences of diffusion of artifacts in the highlands of Oaxaca suggest that intraregional trade was a basic means of integrating specialized local economies as early as 1000 B.C. Small ceremonial centers, usually considered to be prima facie evidence of redistributional systems, date from about the same time. However, really large ceremonial centers, such as Monte Alban, first appeared about five centuries later. The rugged highlands had many different econiches formed by abrupt differences of altitude, wind patterns, and soil. Markets provided an easy means of exchanging the specialized products of different econiches, allowing each to specialize in producing the best local goods, and allowing all to enjoy the immense variety of goods produced in the area. Regional and local markets have continued to flourish to the present time.

Long-distance trade became increasingly important after the development of states in the Mexican area. Mayan traders travelled great distances by land and by sea along the coasts. Olmec traders may have established bases as far away as the coast of Ecuador. And the Pochteca, long-distance traders of

12. Gamst argues that Ethiopia is an even better example than Egypt of an agrarian state without urbanism. F. C. Gamst, "Peasantries and Elites without Urbanism: The Civilization of Ethiopia," *Comparative Studies in Society and History* 12 (1970):372-92.

the Aztec state, traveled great distances by land to other states. As in the case of Mesopotamian states, these long-distance traders were agents of royalty. But further, the Pochteca were spies and decoys whose duties included the subversion of neighboring states which were objectives of Aztec imperialism.

Conquest was another important means of integrating different communities and economies into centralized systems. Mexican states engaged in warfare for this purpose and for the purpose of exacting tribute. Peruvian and Bolivian states were similarly involved in conquest. A series of states centered in the highlands of Peru, which culminated in the Incan state of the Quechuan peoples, developed large empires whose economies were largely based on the tribute of conquered peoples. The state collected all surplus as tribute and redistributed it. The economy of the Inca empire was more closely controlled than the economies of other New World empires. Trade played a much smaller role than in the economy of the Aztec empire. Markets served more the function of social communication than of the exchange of goods.

Centers of redistribution and centers of trade were often distinct in East Asian and Southeast Asian states. Both types of urban centers developed rather late in Southeast Asia and at about the same time (second century B.C.). Funan, the earliest known state, had both types of cities. Vyadupura, the capital, was the redistributive center of a rice-tribute state and of an empire of lesser states that paid tribute in precious goods and slaves. Go-Oceo, the seaport of Funan, was a center for trade of goods from distant places such as other Southeast Asian states, China, Japan, India, Arabia, Greece, and Rome. In later centuries, the states of Southeast Asia tended to specialize in one type of city or the other. For example, the cities of Malay states were primarily trading centers, and the cities of the Khmers were primarily centers of redistribution. Both types of states were deeply involved in developing imperial systems based on conquest.

In Japan, urbanism began even later than in Southeast Asia and coincident with the introduction of wet rice agriculture from China. As in Southeast Asia, the centralizing mechanisms of economic exchange varied from town to town. Some were centers of trade, others were centers of redistribution. The primary function of other centers was less economic than political and administrative, recalling the most common type of Chinese city, which was first a residence for a representative of the imperial government, secondarily a place for his civil administrators and a class of literati, and incidentally the locale of industries that serviced the needs of these officials.

Centralized administrative hierarchies are one of the most important features of states and of societies with urban centers. How do these administrative hierarchies develop? Julian Steward and Karl Wittfogel have suggested that large-scale irrigation requires coordination of effort of peoples of many communities and thereby leads naturally to the development of hierarchies of administrative control.[13] Natural watercourses must be altered or dammed; artificial watercourses surveyed and dug; access to water controlled; and the whole system of irrigation maintained so that it is not clogged with debris and silt. These tasks require overall supervision, it has been argued; and since large irrigation systems serve many villages, a supra-village authority must be established. Once the supra-village authority over irrigation has been established, it may acquire control over other aspects of social life. This is the so-

13. J. H. Steward, "Cultural Causality and Law," *American Anthropologist* 51(1949):1-27; K. A. Wittfogel, *Oriental Despotism: A Comparative Study of Total Power* (New Haven: Yale University Press, 1957).

called hydraulic hypothesis. Robert Mc-Adams and others claim that it has been disproved by archaeological evidence in Peru and Mesopotamia, where large-scale irrigation systems followed rather than preceded the development of states.[14] Moreover, Edmund R. Leach has shown that in the case of Sri Lanka very-large-scale irrigation systems were constructed and maintained without the benefit of centralized administrative hierarchies.[15] That large-scale irrigation systems are the only direct cause of centralization of political regimes is obviously not true. But as Robert Murphy and William Mitchell have noted, the real problem is our mechanistic model of causality which leads us to search for a single cause that precedes the effect.[16] Increased centralization in the organization of any set of activities surely would provide impetus for greater centralization in the organization of other sets of activities in society. Activities related to hydraulic works are but one set of such activities that can add to or be affected by an impetus towards centralized organization.

CONCLUSION

Welcome to urban anthropology—with a vengeance! We hope that you can now see what it means to take the archaeological record seriously. We have tried to sort out the variety of paths to urbanism that have been hypothesized by archaeologists and anthropologists, and you can see that we know at least that the picture is not simple. The rudimentary outlines seem clear: food-production increases are associated with the introduction and development of domesticated plants. These, in turn, are associated with the development of nucleated settlements. Specialization and integration are associated with the development of political organization, which, in turn, foments the development of larger scale economic regimes.

But within this outline there is much room for differing lines of development The picture is not clear yet; we have much to learn.

For Further Reading

Hole, F. "Investigating the Origins of Mesopotamian Civilization." *Science* 153(3736)(5 August 1966):605-11. A somewhat more moderate view of the "Temple-city" of Mesopotamia than is presented in this chapter.

Polanyi, K. et al. *Trade and Market in the Early Empires: Economics in History and Theory.* Glencoe: The Free Press, 1957. Still the best treatment of economic systems in early states.

Price, B. *Mesoamerica: The Evolution of Civilization.* New York: Random House, 1968. A good regional synthesis.

Wolf, E. R. *Peasants.* Englewood Cliffs: Prentice-Hall, 1966. Wolf argues that peasants may exist in states without multifunctional cities.

Bibliography

Adams, R. McC. 1966. *The Evolution of Urban Society: Early Mesopotamia and Prehispanic Mexico.* Chicago: Aldine Publishing Company.

Childe, V. G. 1950. "The Urban Revolution." *Town Planning Review* 21:3-17.

14. C. H. Kraeling and R. McC. Adams, eds., *City Invincible: A Symposium on Urbanization and Cultural Development in the Ancient Near East* (Chicago: University of Chicago Press, 1960).

15. E. R. Leach, "Hydraulic Society in Ceylon," *Past and Present* 15(1959):-2-26.

16. R. Murphy, "Culture Change," in *Biennial Review of Anthropology,* ed. B. J. Siegel and A. R. Beals (Stanford: Stanford University Press, 1967); W. P. Mitchell, "The Hydraulic Hypothesis: A Reappraisal," *Current Anthropology* 14(1973):532-34.

Lathrap, D. 1970. *The Upper Amazon*. New York: Praeger Publishers.

Mitchell, W. P. 1973. "The Hydraulic Hypothesis: A Reappraisal." *Current Anthropology* 14:532-34.

Service, E. R. 1962. *Primitive Social Organization: An Evolutionary Perspective*. New York: Random House.

Wheatley, P. *The Pivot of the Four Quarters: A Preliminary Enquiry Into the Origins and Character of the Ancient Chinese City*. Chicago: Aldine Publishing Co., 1971.

Wittfogel, K. A. 1957. *Oriental Despotism: A Comparative Study of Total Power*. New Haven: Yale University Press.

3 | Urban Places of Different Cultures

PREINDUSTRIAL CITIES

Some social scientists are preoccupied with models of progress which they imagine are analogous to the evolutionary theory of biologists.[1] Evolutionary theory in biology, of course, is not a statement about progress. It is a statement about the *processes of change and differentiation* of populations of life forms. Only in the most vague sense—changes in the range of possible new forms in particular lines—is it exemplary of linear models of reality in Western folk cosmologies. The "evolutionary" models of progress fashioned by social scientists are very different from the evolutionary theory of biology. They serve as excellent examples of the Western penchant for linear models of reality.[2] One such model of progress that masquerades as an evolutionary model is a linear arrangement of types of cities from primitive to modern—preindustrial, industrial, postindustrial. Gideon Sjoberg's model of the preindustrial city implies the whole typology, and it is the most widely cited model of premodern cities.

According to Sjoberg, preindustrial cities all around the world are pretty much the same. They have commercial, political, educational, and religious functions, sometimes specializing in one or another of these. Typically, the population of the preindustrial city is very small in comparison to the

total population of its hinterland (less than 10 percent of the total population), and population growth of such a city is mostly by accretion. Here methods of agriculture, storage, and transport are inefficient, and mechanization is virtually unknown. Surpluses of food produced by the whole society are too small to support larger urban populations. Rigid segregation characterizes the social system of preindustrial cities; different wards or quarters of the city are inhabited by different occupational and ethnic groups. Neighborhoods are communities in which primary relationships predominate, and land use is not really specialized. In preindustrial cities workshops are located within residential buildings, and temples serve as schools and market centers. There is an absence of industrialism. Production in the city as in the country is dependent on animal power, and it is not specialized. Workmen produce whole objects. Production of different kinds of goods and services is in the hands of occupational associations or guilds that recruit new mem-

1. Models of progress are teleological rather than evolutionary.
2. *See* D. Lee, "Linear Models of Reality," in *Every Man His Way: Readings in Cultural Anthropology,* ed. A. Dundes (Englewood Cliffs: Prentice-Hall, 1968).

bers primarily on the basis of relationships such as kinship. Methods of production are not standardized, and goods are not sorted by standard. Prices are not standard, but arrived at by haggling. Even money itself may not be standardized.

Sjoberg says that the population of the preindustrial city is divided into three strata. The most respected and powerful stratum is that of the literate elite, which consists of the leaders of governmental, religious, and educational institutions, and the owners of large amounts of land. The urban masses comprise a lower stratum that produces goods and services for the benefit of the literate elite. Outcastes—slaves, beggars, entertainers, and sometimes merchants—are members of the least regarded stratum.

The family is a vigorous institution in preindustrial cities. Extended families of several generations and with many members living in a single household are common. Inheritance is through males, and according to the rule of primogeniture. Females are considered inferior and kept secluded. Sjoberg goes so far as to suggest that magic predominates over science or even religion in the cultures of preindustrial cities. And he characterizes these cities as being isolated.

Sjoberg's model of the preindustrial city is attractive because it is so straightforward. But our knowledge of cities and the process of urbanization has grown greatly since Sjoberg's work, and we have to take this new knowledge into account. As a result, we can level many criticisms at the model and develop it in detail much more than before.

One problem with the model is familiar: it is ethnocentric in the sense that it is based on the stone cities of Europe, the Near East, and China. But there are examples of cities, even in Europe, which are not consistent with that which Sjoberg describes. Feudal Moscow was a loose confederation of semi-autonomous villages, but we think of it as a city. Renaissance Naples was an absolute state, but differed from Sjoberg's model in that the elite were not massed within the walls of the city any more than they were in feudal Moscow.

Sjoberg's model fails even more obviously when it is compared to preindustrial cities of Japan and the New World. In Japan, cities were built around the palace (Kyoto), the fortress of the major warlords (Edo), and the major port of foreign trade (Osaka). In addition, there were many castle towns of minor warlords, market towns, port towns, and post towns. There were few instances of urban centers having multiple functions. The literate elite was an essentially rural population that lived in monastaries and small shrine centers scattered throughout the land. Old Edo of the Tokugawa Shogunate of the seventeenth century was more populous (about one million people) than any city of Europe at that time, but it had no literate elite.[3] Even more striking examples of preindustrial cities without literate elites are to be found in the illiterate high civilizations of pre-Columbian Peru and Bolivia.

These cities differ from Sjoberg's model of the preindustrial city because they rapidly fluctuate in population. Many pre-Columbian urban centers were essentially empty except on set market days and days of ritual observances. Spanish colonial officials imposed the architecture of the Western stone city on Latin America—the municipal form with town houses, municipal palace, central cathedral, and great square—but the Indians of Latin America have been slow to change their habit of occasional urbanism. They go to cities for festivals and periodic

3. R. J. Smith, "Town and City in Pre-Modern Japan: Small Families, Small Households, and Residential Instability," in *Urban Anthropology: Cross-Cultural Studies of Urbanization,* ed. A. Southall (New York: Oxford University Press, 1973).

markets. This phenomenon is especially apparent in Guatemala, where Indians comprise a large proportion of the total population.

Still another feature implied by Sjoberg's model that does not fit many empirical instances is that of discontinuity between urban and rural populations. The architectural manifestations of that discontinuity is the protective wall of the stone city. Some pre-Columbian cities of the New World were "green cities." That is, population density did not suddenly increase and agricultural activity cease as one passed from the countryside into the urban realm. Density increased gradually as farm plots became smaller and much less common. The best-known example is the Toltecan city of Teotihuacan, near present-day Mexico City, which in the fourth century was the most populous (400,000 people) city in the world. Although Teotihuacan was densely populated, corn and other food crops were planted in small plots throughout the city. It had no protective walls, although Toltecs were occasionally engaged in warfare with their neighbors. The city was built, not around a central square, but on a carefully planned grid of streets that intersected at right angles and which, in total, covered almost thirty square kilometers. Temples lined the avenues to the most important shrines—referred to now as the Pyramid of the Sun and the Pyramid of the Moon. Regularly placed enclosures were devoted to residential housing, manufacture of goods, and markets. The arrangements were neither like those of the medieval stone city of the West nor of its prototype, the marketless city of Mesopotamia. Social strata existed at Teotihuacan, but they were probably within the context of corporate kin groups, conical clans such as the *calpulli* of the Aztec within which clan segments were distinguished as junior or senior branches. These may have approximated the Mesopotamian parish corporations, but would have been very different from the class structure described in Sjoberg's model of the preindustrial city.[4]

Yoruba towns in West Africa will serve as a final example of the inadequacy of Sjoberg's model, though it may be an unfair example.[5] Yoruba towns are not urban centers if you insist that to qualify as an urban center a place must have as inhabitants a majority who are not agriculturists. Even in Ibadan (population more than one million—density almost fifty thousand per square mile) a majority of the inhabitants are farmers; and in the smaller towns, the percentage of farmers in the urban population is often about 80 percent. What is more, very large percentages of the Yoruba live in towns. In Ibadan Province about 60 percent of the Yoruba live in towns with populations greater than twenty thousand.[6] Populations of towns have grown rapidly since the early nineteenth century, but towns of fifty thousand population or more have probably existed since before the twelfth century.

Size and density of the populations of Yoruba towns easily qualifies them as urban centers. The percentage of town dwellers in the total population even approaches—perhaps surpasses—the standard of industrial cities. Everywhere in Yoruba kingdoms the percentage of town dwellers is greater than the 10 percent stipulated for preindustrial cities by Sjoberg.

Why do Yoruba towns have so many farmers inhabiting them? First, farmlands lie on the peripheries of the towns and are within daily walking distance of the towns of less than twenty-five thousand population. Farmers of larger towns whose fields

4. R. McC. Adams, *The Evolution of Urban Society: Early Mesopotamia and Prehispanic Mexico* (Chicago: Aldine Publishing Co., 1966), p. 88; and E. R. Wolf, *Sons of Shaking Earth* (Chicago: University of Chicago Press, 1959), p. 136.

5. P. C. Lloyd, "The Yoruba: An Urban People?" in Southall *Urban Anthropology*.

6. Ibid., p. 108.

are not nearby spend part of their time—from weekends to most of the growing season—in rural hamlets near their fields. Such hamlets have no political autonomy. The most distant fields of the largest towns, such as Ibadan, are less than thirty miles away.

Men are the farmers. Their wives are traders who usually remain in town. Polygamy is fairly common and may be more tolerable in situations where the man is occasionally away farming or one of the wives is occasionally away trading. Land is held by corporate descent groups. Members of a descent group do not cooperate in their labors; the group merely holds land in trust. Each male member is entitled to work as much land as he needs, but no more. The women are organized into trade guilds that protect their members from sharp practices of others, but each woman is an independent trader. Much of the trading is in cooked foods which are often less expensive than cooking one's own. Both men and women produce craft goods. There are craft guilds, but one can change guilds almost at will. Yoruba markets are very large, but there is very little overall organization.

Class structure in the Western sense hardly exists. Males are born into descent groups of more or less equal status and gain respect as they grow older. Land cannot be inherited or acquired beyond one's own ability to work it. Few traders inherit wealth from their parents. Wealth is gained by farming and trading. Leadership titles are gained by open competition with others of one's own descent group. The rich and powerful among the Yoruba confer much less advantage to their children for achieving wealth and power than do the rich and powerful among Europeans. Domestic slaves were common before the colonial period in Yoruba towns.

Each Yoruba town was founded by a king whose line is sacred. Kings have councils of chieftans who are heads of the different descent groups. The king's palace and compound with its central market forms the center of town. Compounds of the different descent groups of the town surround the palace and market. Roads radiate from the market, pass through the town wall and beyond to rural hamlets and other towns.

Clearly, Sjoberg did not have Yoruba towns in mind when he devised his model of the preindustrial city. But the Yoruba town is a very exceptional case that perhaps will never fit any model of urbanism.

Redfield and Singer[7] arrange four types of cities along a continuum from most primitive to most modern, as follows: (1) cities of literati and native bureaucrats; (2) cities of native entrepreneurs; (3) cities of the worldwide managers and entrepreneurs; and (4) cities of the new bureaucracies. The Industrial Revolution is supposed to separate (1) and (2) from (3) and (4).

Cities of literati and native bureaucrats are centers of learning and authority that change implicit "little traditions" of folk in their hinterlands into explicit and systematic "great traditions." Other types of cities absorb the traditions of foreign culture that disintegrate local moral norms and foster the free development of economic, political, and intellectual life. This transformation of the moral order spreads then to the hinterlands, pushing aside the local urbanizing culture that had begun previously to spread into rural areas. Such cities have as frequent social types ". . . businessmen, administrators alien to those they administer, and rebels, reformers, planners and plotters of many varieties."[8]

Redfield and Singer pursue this line of differentiation by distinguishing between primary urbanization and secondary urbanization. Primary urbanization is the process by which local traditions are transformed

7. Redfield and Singer, "The Cultural Role of Cities," *Economic Development and Cultural Change* 3(1)(1954):53-73.

8. Ibid., p. 59.

into native civilizations. Secondary urbanization occurs when a native civilization encounters other, stronger civilizations and is partly destroyed and later reformed as a secular or cosmopolitan civilization.

What is perhaps surprising about this formulation is that it seems almost to explain the types of cities and changes that occurred in urban localities of Southeast Asia from the fifth century through the mid-nineteenth century. The very first evidences of cities in the area are from the second century B.C. From the beginning, there seem to have been two major types of city: (1) cities whose economic basis was rice tribute from a surrounding hinterland; and (2) cities whose economic basis was long-distance trade between India and China. The earliest known state, Funan (in present-day Cambodia), had both types of city as did many states that evolved later. But some states had one or the other type of city. At first blush, the rice-tribute states appear to be examples of Redfield and Singer's type (1), which includes cities of literati and native bureaucracy. And the cities of trade appear to correspond with their type (2), which includes cities of native commerce. Even more interesting is the fact that although there were individual exceptions, cities of trade gained great predominance over rice-tribute states during the period from the fifth to the twelfth century. The earliest state, Funan, fell at the end of the fifth century, and although most of the successor states of Funan in mainland Southeast Asia were rice-tribute states with capital cities, these were overshadowed by powerful cities of trade that developed in the island area of Southeast Asia. So far so good, in the sense that type (2) follows type (1). However, a reverse trend began in the twelfth century, with rapid development of apparent type (1) cities in the mainland states of Burma, Thailand, Cambodia, Laos, and Vietnam. The one major trading state of the mainland, Champa, went into rapid

decline; the most powerful trading state of the islands, SriVijaya, was conquered by a state (Majapahit) that depended on rice tribute as well as trade; and the mainland area, characterized by rice-tribute cities, began to overshadow the islands and their cities of trade. Both types of traditional cities continued essentially unchanged until about the middle of the nineteenth century when European colonial cities began to dominate the area.

INDUSTRIAL CITIES

A model of industrial cities is implied in Redfield and Singer's model of centers of transformation from outside influence. But that model probably refers more to colonial cities and to industrializing cities. The so-called Chicago School, especially Burgess and Parks, developed a much more explicit model of industrial cities based on Chicago in the 1920s.[9] We shall describe it here, not because it is the only model of industrial cities, but because it is the most famous.

Chicago in the 1920s could be viewed as a series of concentric zones. Zone 1 was the central business district which was the focus of commercial, social, and civic life. Department stores, fashion shops, office buildings, clubs, banks, hotels, theaters, and museums dominated this zone. Zone 2 was a transitional zone, with land held by speculators who expected Zone 1 to expand into Zone 2. Most speculators did nothing to improve their property, especially if it was tenements or old hotels, because improvements usually resulted in higher taxes. Rents were relatively cheap and this zone housed the tenderloin or redlight district. Manufacturing and wholesale businesses were common in this zone, too. Zone 3 was a blue-collar residential area. Lower class im-

9. R. E. Park, E. W. Burgess, and R. D. McKenzie, *The City* (Chicago: University of Chicago Press, 1925).

migrants who improved their status moved into this zone from Zone 2. Zone 4 was a better residential area for the middle class. Small businessmen, clerks, salesmen, and some professional people lived in this zone. A few small satellite business centers with a branch bank, drugstore, cafe, and movie house, served the convenience needs of middle-class inhabitants of Zone 4. Zone 5 was the residential zone of the wealthy managers of Zone 1. Zone 6 was an agricultural zone, and Zone 7 included the rest of the city's hinterlands.

The model was applied successfully to most flatland industrial cities in the United States. It did not conform well to European cities. For one thing, Europeans had long favored the central core of the city as a residential zone because of easier access to cultural affairs, shops, and offices. Some residential areas that were near the core of European cities were very high status areas. In America this was reversed to some extent because of the development of automobiles and individual transportation. Only the poor who could not afford an automobile needed to live near public transportation or within walking distance of work.

The automobile changed the shape of American cities, too. After World War II, the United States Congress passed federal legislation that provided funds for developing an interstate highway system. The first parts of the system to be completed were near cities. Coincidentally, other legislation created loan funds that were more easily acquired and used by suburban businessmen. The result was a housing boom in the suburbs, partially underwritten by government-guaranteed mortgages and tax exemptions for interest paid on home mortgages. Hundreds of millions of tax dollars were given in the form of freeways as subsidy to housing contractors and middle-class suburbanites who now drive to work almost as quickly as they did when they lived in Zone 3 or 4. Businesses moved to the suburbs for

the convenience and dollars of the middle class. The small business centers of Zone 4 blossomed into giant shopping centers, with plenty of free parking. Business that remained in the old central core suffered losses. The tax base of the city was undermined by business losses and movement of the middle class to the suburbs.

Beginning several decades earlier, another great change in American society— the mechanization of agriculture—had begun to reach full fruition in the development of agribusiness. This development reached into the Southern states, displacing hundreds of thousands of the rural poor who depended on the sale of their labor for their livelihood. Poor whites and blacks, mostly blacks, migrated from the Southern states into the industrial cities of the North. The blacks entered Zone 2 just as poor European immigrants had before them, and the lower class whites of Zone 2 moved into Zone 3. Workingmen of Zone 3 and the middle class of Zone 4 moved into the suburbs, abandoning the city and taking their tax dollars with them. Zone 2 expanded inward into Zone 1 and outward into Zone 3. Enormous areas of the city became slums. Black resentment increased as fewer tax dollars were available for maintaining urban facilities. More businesses and more of the middle class fled the squalor and crime of the city.

It all seemed to happen too rapidly to avoid the urban crisis of the 1960s in the United States. The crisis is not past. It has just plateaued, and we are becoming accustomed to it. Some remedies are being tried. Abandoned houses in the city are being claimed for taxes by some municipalities and sold at low prices, or are homesteaded to homeowners so they can afford to pay the taxes. A few slums have been razed or transformed into fashionable residential areas, such as Georgetown in Washington D.C. and the Near Northside in Chicago.

Many American cities cannot be described in terms of concentric zones. Another common type is divided into sectors. This type of urban geography was noticed by Homer Hoyt in a WPA survey of 1934.[10] It is a common type in the South where different classes and castes inhabit different quarters of the city. The sectors, whether residential, commercial, or industrial, have tended to grow outward as the city became larger. New highways in Southern cities have tended to modify the sector type of city towards the concentric zone type.

American industrial cities may seem to change much more rapidly than preindustrial cities—to be more dynamic and less static. Partly this is an artifact of more detailed knowledge. As we look back in time, things seem more fixed and less variable—not that they necessarily were. In any case, the rapid change in the macrostructure of American industrial cities warns us to remember that cultures and cultural images, cosmologies, vary from time to time as well as from society to society.

POSTINDUSTRIAL CITIES

Urbanism in this century has culminated in qualitatively new forms of settlement that may be grouped together as modern metropoles. The modern metropolis exists side by side, within the context of the same cultural and social system, with other forms of urbanism. New York, London, Calcutta, Bangkok ,Tokyo, and Rio de Janiero are all different in the details of their structures. Each shares detailed features with cities, towns, and villages of its own cultural and social system. But modern metropoles of different cultures share common features, too. They have in common great population size (more than a million), high population density (sometimes approaching fifty thousand per square mile), and a great dependency not only on their own hinterlands but also on the world economy.

We know very little about the various types of metropoles. They seem to have in common the feature of multiple subcenters. Once it was popular to assume that metropoles in some areas such as the eastern coast of the United States would fuse, creating massive cities hundreds of miles across. That seems not to be happening, because the old centers continue to have contravening commercial and bureaucratic infrastructures that are not easily deposed by new structures. However, their metropolitan areas do continue to grow.

While we have not yet learned how to study the old forms of urbanism satisfactorily, new forms are evolving.

For Further Reading

Harris, C. D. and Ullman, E. L. "The Nature of Cities." Annals of the American Academy of Political Sciences, November 1945. A description of land use patterns organized around functionally distinct nuclei.

Murphey, R. "The City as a Center of Change: Western Europe and China." *Readings in Cultural Geography,* edited by P. C. Wagner and M. W. Mikesell. Chicago: University of Chicago Press, 1962. A balance to the views of Redfield and Singer.

Park, R. E. *Human Communities: The City and Human Ecology.* Glencoe: The Free Press, 1952. Social and cultural mapping of the city.

Wheatley, P. *The Pivot of the Four Quarters: A Preliminary Enquiry into the Origins and Character of the Ancient Chinese City.* Chicago: Aldine Publishing Co., 1971. A very scholarly work on the nature of ancient urbanism on the North China Plain, based on archaeological, literary, and epigraphic sources.

Wheatley, P. "What the Greatness of the City Is Said to Be." *Pacific Viewpoint* 4(1963):

10. H. Hoyt, *The Structure and Growth of Residential Neighborhoods in American Cities* (Federal Housing Authority, 1939).

163-88. A most thorough review of G. Sjoberg's *The Preindustrial City*.

Bibliography

Hoyt, H. 1939. *The Structure and Growth of Residential Neighborhoods in American Cities.* Federal Housing Authority.

Redfield, R., and Singer, M. B. 1954. "The Cultural Role of Cities." *Economic Development and Cultural Change* 3(1):53-73.

Southall, A., ed. 1973. *Urban Anthropology: Cross-Cultural Studies of Urbanization.* New York: Oxford University Press.

4 | Anthropological Views of Urban Sociology

BASIC CONCEPTS

Anthropologists often study societal units, the likes of which they have not seen before. Try to put yourself in the place of an anthropologist arriving in an urban center he is not familiar with, and imagine what you might choose to study. Preparing to go to the field, you will have read everything available about the people you intend to study: reports of missionaries and travelers, the work of other professionals. Likely, you will have formed in advance some notions about the social structures, the groupings, the language, the religion, the etiquette, the economy, and a dozen other categories of the culture of urbanites. And inevitably, those notions will affect what you look for and how you go about looking.

Although archaeologists have been interested in urban places for a good while, only a few ethnologists have shared their interest until recently. Therefore, much of what you read about urban centers will have been written by people in other disciplines, especially sociologists, geographers, and architects. Your reading will have alerted you to the existence of subcultures, neighborhoods and communities, the urban poor and the elites, social problems, spatial distributions of crime and housing, markets and social disorganization. In this chapter, we shall attempt to wade with you through that welter of concepts—evaluating some, placing others in perspective. Our idea is to put our intellectual house more or less in order so that we can proceed to the main task: doing ethnology in urban places.

To begin with, we need some elementary definitions. At least we should agree on what we mean when we talk about "society" and about "culture." The notion of culture is a fairly recent one. Most discussions of definitions of culture begin with Tylor's classic definition less than one hundred years back:

. . . that complex whole which includes knowledge, belief, art, law, morals, custom, and any other capabilities and habits acquired by man as a member of society.[1]

Yet an inventory published in 1952 by Clyde Kluckhohn and Alfred Kroeber[2] revealed several hundred definitions, many conflicting, that have been used since then.

1. E. B. Tylor, *Primitive Culture*, 2 vols. (New York: Harper & Row, Publishers, 1958—first published 1874).

2. A. L. Kroeber and C. Kluckhohn, *Culture: A Critical Review of Concepts and Definitions*, Papers of the Peabody Museum of American Archaeology and Ethnology, vol. 47, no. 1 (Cambridge, Mass.: Harvard University, 1952).

The problem is not that anthropologists do not know what culture is, but that various people need it to be various things. Nobody ever saw, heard, tasted, smelled, or kicked culture. It is a concept we made up to help us think. Therefore, the first requirement of any definition we decide to use is not that it be accurate—because it cannot help being accurate—but that it be useful.[3]

Paul Bohannan has suggested that notions of society and culture are of basically two kinds, depending upon whether one is a social anthropologist (or sociologist) or a cultural anthropologist. The former proceeds from the position that man is a social animal and that culture is the glue that holds society together; the latter proceeds from the view that man is a tool-making animal, that culture is all of his tools, and that society is one of those tools.[4]

Being cultural anthropologists, we see culture as all the "tools," physical or intellectual, that humans devise in order to adapt to the world. *A culture is the tools used by a particular population.* *Society* we shall call one of those tools: the pattern of human interaction. Many writers speak as though "*a society*" were synonymous with "*a population.*" We do not. For us, a society is the pattern of interaction of a population.

Subsets of many populations, while sharing much of the culture of the rest of the population, possess other cultural elements that they share only among themselves. We shall refer to those elements as a subculture. A subculture may or may not include a sub-society; usually it does. Cultures and subcultures, societies, and sub-societies, and even populations, are much easier to define than to identify, as we shall see later on. But for the moment, let's leave the definitions and push on to consider some of the traditional concerns of sociologists studying in urban places, using our definitions as we go.

THE CHICAGO SCHOOL OF SOCIOLOGY

In the United States, perhaps the earliest and most influential group of professionals studying urban places were Park, Burgess, Wirth, and McKenzie—the four horsemen of the University of Chicago's Department of Sociology. Using Chicago as their laboratory, those four and their students set many of the themes that still appear in urban studies, sociological and otherwise. The themes emerging from the Chicago School (as it is sometimes called) that we shall discuss here are social disorganization communities, and neighborhoods, social problems, and (more a subdiscipline than a theme) human ecology.

The Chicago sociologists did not emerge full grown from the egg, and it is well to keep in mind the context from which they developed and within which they operated. It is especially important to remember their predecessors: philanthropic social workers. As Burgess himself points out,

It is important to make clear that the Department of Sociology studies were not the first field studies in Chicago. If you go back as far as 1895, in the Hull-House Papers, you will find urban studies. It would be correct to say that systematic urban studies in Chicago began with these Hull-House studies. . . . the Chicago School of Civics and Philanthropy (later the School of Service Administration of this university), had carried on a series of studies of the immigrant and of the operation of Hull-House. They began these studies as early as 1908.[5]

3. Materialist anthropologists will dispute this statement, but we stand by it.

4. P. Bohannan, "Conscience Collective and Culture," in *Essays on Sociology and Philosophy,* ed., K. H. Wolff (New York: Harper & Row, Publishers, 1964), pp. 77-96.

5. E. W. Burgess and D. J. Bogue, eds., *Urban Sociology* (Chicago: University of Chicago Press, 1967), p. 4.

URBAN ANTHROPOLOGY
Anthropological Views of Urban Sociology

At the turn of the century, Chicago was one of the major locations to which United States industrialists imported cheap labor from Europe. As each wave of immigrants adapted to their new environment, they were replaced by a new wave. After the European pool of cheap labor dried up in 1914, Chicago industrialists turned their eyes south, recruiting poor, mostly rural, blacks and whites from that hinterland. After World War I, with the maturation of United States labor unions and the passage of laws restricting immigration, the labor supply changed drastically. Since cheap labor had become less plentiful, United States industrialists invested in machines. But at the time when the Chicago sociologists and their philanthropic predecessors were formulating their views of urban life, Chicago was witnessing the arrival and assimilation of waves of immigrants.

The early Chicago sociologists were activists. Park, for example, had been a journalist and admired the muckrakers. He appears to have turned to sociology not because of a change of interests but for a change of methodology. From the outset, he and his colleagues and students involved themselves in public and private municipal activities, advising and working in community service centers, conducting and directing censuses, and the like. They took the folk issues of their particular subculture as general sociological issues. The definitions that appear in their writings tend to be folk definitions, their theoretical statements programs for practical action.

HUMAN ECOLOGY

The first practical step in solving a problem is to locate it. In an article published in 1916, Park made a number of suggestions for "investigation of human behavior in the city environment."[6] In Park's view, two aspects of the city were to be studied: the physical and the moral. The former turns out to be primarily economic, dealing with competition, land use, and the like; while the latter is primarily psychological, although it manifests itself in behavior and behavioral labels: family life, prostitution, ethnic groupings, suicide, and others. While the physical aspects of cities have become the domain of "human ecology" (sometimes confused with cultural ecology in anthropology), the remainder has become the subject matter of mainstream sociology, the modifier "urban" having become obsolete.[7]

An important concept in human ecology is the "natural area." A natural area is a locality that, because of physical characteristics, is felt to attract certain members of a population. Presumably, the populations of various areas have distinctive sub-societies. Thus, from the human ecologist's point of view, society is spatially distributed. In practice, the distributions with which human ecologists deal are not populations of humans, but populations of traits, such as age, sex, income, racial membership on the one hand, and incidence of certain kinds of crime, suicide, insanity, and the like on the other. At the same time, selected physical characteristics are enumerated, such as kinds of buildings and uses of land. Natural areas, then, have, in practice, become spatially bounded aggregates (or frequency tables) of physical and behavioral traits.

Early studies in human ecology were limited to map making. Burgess reminisces,

I had students in my course on Social Pathology making maps of all types of social problems for

---

6. R. E. Park, "The City: Suggestions for the Investigation of Human Behavior in the Urban Environment," in *American Journal of Sociology* 20 (1916):577-612.

7. D. White and T. Weaver, "Sociological Contributions to an Urban Anthropology," in *The Anthropology of Urban Environments,* Society for Applied Anthropology (Boulder: University of Colorado Press, 1972), p. 102.

which we could get data. . . . I think the maps of juvenile delinquency were the first ones undertaken. They were followed by maps showing the distribution of the patrons of the public dance halls.[8]

With the perfection of statistical techniques, however, human ecology studies have increasingly relied upon one or another method of correlating one trait or set of traits with another. Crudely stated, the reasoning behind statistical correlations is that when the frequent occurrence of one trait is coincident with the frequent occurrence of another trait, a relationship is felt to exist between them. Notwithstanding the fact that such evidence would be considered circumstantial in a court of law, the technique has proved valuable, for example in establishing a relation between smoking cigarettes and suffering various illnesses. And criticizing it is about like criticizing freeways. Nevertheless, we feel constrained to mention some of the kinds of criticism that have been made.

Weaknesses occur in the technique at two points: selection of data and interpretation of the correlations. Because sociological studies often use surveys of one kind or another, we must discuss theoretical objections to survey research, but that discussion will come in chapter 7. As far as the data are concerned, items selected, even simple ones such as age, sex, and income, do not have meaning within themselves and must be invested with meaning by the social scientist. When more complex traits, such as criminal or psychologically labeled events, are introduced, the problems become manifold. In practice, most sociologists use folk definitions and interpretations of such events. There is nothing wrong, of course, with folk definitions as long as one uses them self-consciously, aware of their influence on the conclusions drawn from completed study. Only recently are some sociologists becoming aware of the implications of arbitrarily labeling various kinds of behavior as deviant. Again, the subjectivity of evaluations is not at issue. All social science requires subjective interpretations. The problem with statistical studies is that the subjectivity is hidden in the data selection, and then the data are reduced to numbers, giving the studies a dangerously false aura of concreteness and objectivity.

When a statistically significant correlation is discovered, interpretation is called for again. The tendency is to suggest that one of the traits *causes* the other. Any time such a statement is made, at least five other interpretations are also possible: the second trait could have caused the first; both could have been caused by a third factor; instead multiple mutual causation could be at work of linear causality, systemically related, (as, for example, we suggested in the case of the development of cities); the co-occurrence of the traits may have happened by chance; or the original interpretations of the data may have dictated that the correlations would occur. Again, these weaknesses do not necessarily constitute grounds for rejecting the technique altogether, but they do suggest that the results of statistical analysis be treated with much more reserve than one normally encounters.

One of the most sophisticated modern instruments used by contemporary practitioners of human ecology is the Shevky-Bell method of classifying urban neighborhoods on the basis of social rank, segregation, and urbanization of the populations. Once neighborhoods are characterized in that manner, various other behavioral traits of the populations, such as the frequency of visiting people nearby, are then recorded (cf Greer 1956). And it is often stated or implied that the first set of traits causes the second. Unfortunately, even such sophisticated delimi-

8. Burgess and Bogue, *Urban Sociology*, pp. 3, 5-6.

tation of natural areas appears increasingly crude the more one knows about the subculture of the population involved. Or, as White and Weaver put it, "The greater the extent of cultural data, the less adequate the ecological accommodation in terms of theory."[9]

Before leaving the discussion of human ecology, we should acknowledge that we have not mentioned the most primitive fallacy of human ecology: the notion that subcultures are always in bounded spaces. We have neglected it for two reasons—first, because the criticism seems obvious; second, because we think that it is irrelevant. If our contention is correct, that the original purpose of human ecology was to locate social problems so that they could be solved, and if the most practical kind of location for purposes of applying solutions was a spatial one, then the spatial bias was inescapable.

SOCIAL PROBLEMS

Not surprisingly, most of the social "problems" were found to be located in areas where traits such as "low income," "deteriorating housing," and "immigrant" occurred frequently. The general explanation of that state of affairs was that life in the city—as opposed to life in rural places—was charac-

terized by *secondary* relationships, rather than by *primary* relationships, and that this condition was responsible for *social disorganization* and *anomie*. Seldom does one find rigorous definitions for the expressions that are italicized in the previous sentence, but the first two at least are easily understood.

Consider a day in which you must interact with, say five people. Assume that the kinds of relationships you have with those five people are of the following kind:

a. kinsperson
b. neighbor
c. workmate
d. person with whom you must deal for economic reasons (e.g., a clerk, a bureaucrat, a bank teller).

Assume, further, that with any given person, you may have more than one kind of relationship. For example, your brother may be your workmate. Assume, finally, that Table 1 summarizes the relationships you have with your five people. We might diagram the relationships as shown in Figure 4.1 on page 33, with each connecting line standing for a different kind of relationship.

9. White and Weaver, "Sociological Contributions," p. 103.

Table 1

PRIMARY AND SECONDARY RELATIONSHIPS

Person Number	Types of Relationships
1	a, b, c, d
2	b, c, d
3	c, d
4	d
5	d (like 4, but you deal only indirectly, through the mail, the telephone, or human intermediaries)

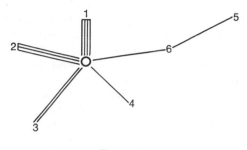

Figure 4.1
PRIMARY AND SECONDARY
RELATIONSHIPS

Now, depending on who is doing the defining and why, the people you have primary relationships with are either 1 through 3, or 1 and 2, with the others being secondary relationships. (We shall return to these ideas while discussing network analysis in chapters 6 and 7.)

What is meant by "social disorganization" and *anomie* is more difficult to untangle. Neither expression can be separated from biases in favor of a romanticized view of rural life and against the urban poor. To complicate matters further, "social disorganization," though a social concept, has strong psychological implications. Often, it is pictured to be either analogous to psychological disorganization or to its cause or its effect. "Social disorganization" is felt to manifest itself socially in the dissolution of the family and other institutions, and otherwise in behavior that has been labeled deviant. Thus, prostitution, street crime, street drunkenness, certain kinds of psychoses, suicide, and indigence are spoken of as indices of social disorganization. (Significantly, private alcoholism, embezzlement, and exploitation of employees are seldom or never included in the trait lists that identify localities suffering from social disorganization.)

When "social disorganization" is treated as the cause of mental disorganization, the psychological condition often is called *ano-*

mie. Among sociologists in the United States, *anomie* most commonly is treated as a condition resulting from one's lack of means to achieve goals. Such a definition oversimplifies and distorts the concept as it was developed by the great French sociologist, Emile Durkheim. At the same time, it diminishes the concept's value regarding "social disorganization," because the lack of means does not necessarily imply "social disorganization." Theoretically oriented sociologists such as Talcott Parsons and Robert Merton have given more sophisticated treatments of the concept, Parsons focusing on the lack of correspondence between an individual's goals and the norms and values of his or her society, and Merton, without making an explicit definition, treating *anomie* as a condition arising from the distortion of either goals or means.[10]

For many anthropologists who follow the principle of cultural relativity—that is, that cultural phenomena may be judged only in terms of the culture or subculture in which they occur—the whole notion of "social disorganization" is problematic. A major activity of ethnographers, of course, is to describe the societies of the populations they study. Following our definition that a society is the pattern of relationships between members of a population, we may say that "social organization" is a description of that pattern. Logically, it follows that if there is no pattern (i.e. if there is *dis*organization) there is no society, and a description is impossible. By definition, all societies are organized.

The only way out of that trap is to say that a society is *relatively* disorganized—relative, that is, to some other society. Discovery of just what that other society is would tell us much about what sociologists

10. R. C. Hinkle, Jr., "Durkheim in American Sociology," in *Essays on Sociology and Philosophy,* ed., K. H. Wolff (New York: Harper & Row Publishers, 1964), pp. 282-83.

really mean when they speak of "social disorganization." But sociologists do not make their bases of comparison explicit. It is up to us to infer them. One such comparative base, especially for the early Chicago sociologists, appears to be an image of a kind of Rousseauean romantic rural society (RRRS), characterized by primary relationships and other social characteristics of many small populations. The comparison is supposedly historical. Recall that the people with social problems in Chicago at the turn of the century were recent arrivals, either from outside the nation or from rural areas of the United States. The idea was that these good folks had gotten their RRRS's disorganized upon moving to the city. Unfortunately, little attempt was ever made to find out if their home societies were really RRRS's.

Essentially the same criticism may be leveled at the sociological practice of labeling as "pathological" the behavior that is supposed to indicate "social disorganization." Every anthropologist is aware that what is pathological in one culture may well be normal in another. In a sense, what is normal might be treated as a question of frequency of occurrence. If a certain kind of behavior occurs frequently enough, it cannot be considered pathological in the culture or subculture where it occurs. Most anthropologists also treat any given culture or subculture as the solution that the population has evolved for coping with the particular environment in which they find themselves. Following that assumption, if we find that one population set labels as pathological, behavior that is normative for another set of the same population, we assume that the labeling serves some purpose.

Every group in society goes about evaluating and labeling the behavior of other groups. What is perfectly normal and natural for group A may be seen as pathologically criminal by group B, and vice versa. Things that we see as strange, exotic, and remote, are generally regarded as dangerous, and we label them so, defining the behavior as deviant. People who do things like that are themselves dangerous and deviant. But the definition of deviance is not a parlor game, because some groups have the power to impose their definitions about *what* is deviant, and *who* is deviant on others. And generally those with political clout or those with disproportionate access to wealth are the imposers. Those without power or wealth are their victims, even though the victimized population does not share these definitions. And finally, one of the major problems of the study of social pathology lies in the enshrinement of official labels, not only by the victim, the policeman, the judge, or the industrialist, but also by the *sociologist.*

Clearly, it would be a violation of our own principle of cultural relativity to evaluate labeling negatively (or otherwise). However, if it is true that sociologists are using a particular set of folk labels, then we are justified in wondering why they do it.

We feel that the most important reason for making one subculture's folk labels the official labels is to achieve the social control of a subordinate population. The labeling not only provides a program of social control but it also cloaks the controllers in an aura of benevolent humanist concern for those they are controlling. This is the very essence of philanthropy.

In small populations, where primary relationships are felt to predominate, the reasoning goes, one behaves "correctly" because he or she is usually under surveillance. In a large population, that effect is diluted because of one's relative anonymity. *The* problem, then, which subsumes almost all of the sociologists' social problems, is how to make people, particularly poor people, behave according to the norms of the sociologist's subculture.

COMMUNITIES, NEIGHBORHOODS, AND "NEIGHBORING"

After the use of police, the most venerable solution has been to promote primary relationships in the city. It is no accident that philanthropic enterprises such as Hull House in Chicago focus upon creating a "community" within a particular locality. Nor is it accidental that many sociologists remain preoccupied with how much contiguous people "neighbor" with each other. Speaking about England, Norman Dennis[11] has suggested that the reason sociologists and social workers have concentrated on the neighborhood (and the reason that foundations and governments have funded them) is that such studies have not disturbed established interests in society one whit. It is much safer to establish a clean-up, paint-up program in the ghetto than it is to change the social and political (capitalist) structure that created the ghetto in the first place. And such a program lets powerful groups sleep much better at night, knowing that the morning will bring social improvement, and little or no change in the social and economic arrangements.

It is interesting to note, while on the subject of English studies, that the English government's response to the threat of a centrally concentrated urban poor has been to build suburban "housing estates" and move poor people out to them. The irony of such a policy—if we accept the rationale of the primary relationship solution—is that studies by Elizabeth Bott,[12] Peter Townsend,[13] Willmott and Young,[14] Young and Willmott,[15] and others indicate that social interaction among the poor in London is more dominated by primary relationships than is social interaction among the so-called middle class.

This does not necessarily mean that relationships among the poor in cities in the United States are of the same kind. And in fact it might be argued that the "social disorganization" syndrome that has preoccu-

pied sociologists in the United States, even if one accepts their formulation, applies not to peculiarly urban events, but to general human responses to change, either economic or (in the case of rural and foreign immigrants to the city) environmental. In 1938, Louis Wirth postulated a peculiar urban "way of life," generated by the independent variables with which he defined "a city": permanence of the settlement and size, density, and heterogeneity of the population. Wirth's formulation portrayed urban life in essentially the same terms that his colleagues had used fifteen years earlier; and he suggested that the urban way of life was to be contrasted with the rural. His purpose was to provide a set of hypotheses about urban life that could be tested by future researchers. In 1951, however, he was to lament that "evidence has not been accumulated in such a fashion as to test any major hypothesis that has been proposed."[16] In chapter 6, we shall discuss theoretical formulations and research by the anthropologist Robert Redfield and his students and critics. With the exception of that work, mostly by anthropologists, Wirth's 1951 statement remains valid today.

One of the brighter spots in the sociological treatment of urban places is the

11. N. Dennis, "The Popularity of the Neighborhood Community Idea," *Readings in Urban Sociology*, ed. R. E. Pahl (London: Pergamon Press, 1968), p. 91.

12. E. Bott, *Family and Social Network: Roles, Norms, and External Relationships in Ordinary Urban Families* (London: Tavistock, 1957).
send,[13] Willmott and Young,[14] Young and

13. P. Townsend, *The Family Life of Old People* (London: Routledge and Kegan Paul, 1957).

14. P. Willmott and M. Young, *Family and Class in a London Suburb* (London: Routledge and Kegan Paul, 1960).

15. M. Young and P. Willmott, *Family and Kinship in East London* (London: Routledge and Kegan Paul, 1957).

16. L. Wirth, "Urbanism as a Way of Life," in *American Journal of Sociology* 44(1939):1-24.

community study. Modeled on anthropological techniques of ethnographic description, community studies have been conducted primarily in smaller towns or within localities in cities. White and Weaver list some of the better known community studies as follows:

Some of the classic small-town studies in the United States include Lynd and Lynd on Middletown (1929), Davis and Dollard on the southern town (1940), Drake and Cayton on black metropolis on the North (1945), West (pseudonym of Withers) on Plainville (1947), Vidich and Bensman on the small town in mass society (1958), and Gallaher's (an anthropologist) restudy of Plainville (1961). Studies on larger cities . . . include Whyte (1955) and Gans (1962) on Boston's Italian district, Amory (1947) on the proper Bostonians, Dobriner (1958) and Gans (1967) on the suburb. The subcultural studies in larger urban areas have often paralleled the social area studies of the urban ecologists, such as Wirth (1928) and Duncan and Duncan (1957) on the black ghetto.[17]

We shall delay discussion of the theoretical and methodological considerations of this kind of study until chapter 7. For the moment it is enough to notice that the most general criticism of this kind of work (aside from Dennis' remarks cited earlier) is that leveled during the past few years at many ethnographies, particularly studies of peasant villages in Latin America: that is, that the villages are treated as societal isolates rather than being placed within the regional and national systems of which they are a part. Such a deficiency is doubly evident in the case of studies of enclaves in the city in the absence of any coherent theory of cities as a whole.

POWER STRUCTURES

Studies of power structures of cities are a special type of partial community study that we find especially attractive as a means of integrating urban situated ethnographies. There is a long tradition in European urban studies of analyzing urban culture as a structure composed of institutions.[18] Sociologists in the United States, as we have seen, have shown little interest in that kind of analysis, although it is an important research tool of many anthropologists. The better studies of power structures in cities come closer than any other kind of sociological endeavor in the United States to providing a general view of all the institutions of the city.

Unfortunately, students of urban power structures spent a number of years fighting each other over method. The two major competing methods were (1) asking a number of people who the local leaders are and tabulating their responses (whom to ask is, of course, a problem), or (2) analyzing sit-

17. White and Weaver, "Sociological Contributions," p. 104; R. S. Lynd and H. M. Lynd, *Middletown, A Study in American Culture* (New York: Harcourt, Brace, 1929); A. Davis and J. Dollard, *Children of Bondage* (Washington, D.C.: American Council on Education, 1940); St. C. Drake and H. R. Cayton, *Black Metropolis* (New York: Harcourt, Brace and World, 1945); J. West, *Plainsville, U.S.A.* (New York: Columbia University Press, 1947); A. J. Vidich and J. Bensman, *Small Town in Mass Society* (Princeton: Princeton University Press, 1958); A. Gallaher, Jr., *Plainville Fifteen Years Later* (New York: Columbia University Press, 1961); W. F. Whyte, *Street Corner Society* (2d edition) (Chicago: University of Chicago Press, 1955); H. J. Gans, *The Urban Villagers* (New York: Free Press, 1962); C. Amory, *The Proper Bostonians* (New York: E. P. Dutton & Co., 1947); W. M. Dobriner, *The Suburban Community* (New York: G. P. Putnam's Sons, 1958); H. J. Gans, *The Levittowners: Way of Life and Politics in a New Suburban Community* (New York: Pantheon Books, 1967); L. Wirth, *The Ghetto* (Chicago: University of Chicago Press, 1928); and O. D. Duncan and B. Duncan, *The Negro Population of Chicago: A Study of Residential Succession* (Chicago: University of Chicago Press, 1957).

18. M. Weber (D. Martindale and G. Neuwirth, trans.), *The City* (New York: Free Press, 1958).

uations in which major decisions are made to find out who is making the decisions. The folly of excluding either technique becomes obvious when one realizes that the kind of power structure found tends to depend on the method used. The more thoroughgoing studies, such as that conducted by Freedman and his colleagues in Syracuse, use both methods.

For Further Reading

Burgess, E. W., and Bogue, D. J., eds. *Urban Sociology.* Chicago: The University of Chicago Press, 1967. A retrospective consideration of the Chicago School by many of its products.

Mills, C. Wright. *The Sociological Imagination.* New York: Oxford University Press, 1959. A more thorough exploration of problems of sociological formulations than we have given —and from a sociologist.

Bibliography

Duncan, O. D., and Duncan, B. 1957. *The Negro Population of Chicago: A Study of Residential Succession.* Chicago: University of Chicago Press.

Pahl, R. E. ed. 1968. *Readings in Urban Sociology.* London: Pergamon Press.

Weber, M. 1958. *The City.* Translated by D. Martindale and G. Neuwirth. New York: Free Press.

White, D., and Weaver, T. 1972. "Sociological Contributions to An Urban Anthropology." In *The Anthropology of Urban Environments,* Society for Applied Anthropology Monograph number 11. Edited by T. Weaver and D. White. Boulder: University of Colorado Press.

5 | Notes on Problems of Complexity and Scale

ETHNOGRAPHIC TECHNIQUES AND COMPLEX SOCIETIES

It should be clear from the preceding chapter that we feel that sociology has, in the main, failed to provide the kinds of studies in and of urban places that we, as anthropologists, find desirable and useful. (The kind of sociology we have criticized is what C. Wright Mills has called "abstracted empiricism.") We have suggested, moreover, that this is an ethical as well as an academic problem. The questions now are, "How can anthropologists do better"? and "How can one go about doing anthropology in urban places"? The later is a common question, one that has received considerable attention in professional journals and symposia. Indeed, a disproportionately large number of articles published by anthropologists who have studied in cities are discussions of which techniques should be followed.[1]

The problems most commonly discussed are those of size, scale, and complexity of urban societies (as we defined those terms at the beginning of chapter 2). The assumption, explicit or implicit, usually is that such problems are not encountered in the study of rural populations or their cultures. Also implied is the notion that techniques of anthropological research that were developed mainly during rural research—be they un-

structured participant observation or the more formally described methods of ethnoscience and cognition—may not be appropriate in large, dense, culturally heterogeneous populations. Proposed corrective measures range from use of census and other survey data to the utilization of multidisciplinary research teams. In this chapter, we shall explore those ideas, primarily examining basic assumptions. In the next chapter, we shall discuss the kinds of research that

1. *See,* for example, R. G. Fox, "Rational and Romance in Urban Anthropology," *Urban Anthropology* 1(1972):205-33; J. James, " 'On the Block': Urban Research Perspectives," *Urban Anthropology* 1(1972):125-40; A. Leeds, "The Anthropology of Cities: Some Methodological Issues," in *Urban Anthropology,* Southern Anthropological Society Proceedings, no. 2, ed. E. Eddy (Athens, Georgia: University of Georgia Press, 1968), pp. 31-47; A. Leeds, "The Significant Variables Determining the Character of Squatter Settlements," *America Latina* 12(1969):44-86; L. Plotnicov, "Anthropological Field Work in Modern and Local Urban Contexts," *Urban Anthropology* 2(1973):248-64; T. Weaver and D. White, "Anthropological Approaches to Urban and Complex Society," in *The Anthropology of Urban Environments,* Society for Applied Anthropology Monograph Series, Monograph no. 11, ed. T. Weaver and D. White (Boulder: Society for Applied Anthropology, 1972), pp. 109-26. Also, implicitly, all the articles in G. M. Foster and R. V. Kemper, eds., *Anthropologists in Cities* (Boston: Little, Brown & Co., 1974) are concerned with methodology.

has been conducted in urban places by anthropologists. Then, in chapter 7, we shall set out for your evaluation a few ideas about research techniques that we feel to be particularly well suited for urban studies by anthropologists.

First, some of the notions just mentioned need to be examined critically. Recall that we have distinguished between size and density of populations and the more inclusive notion of the *scale* of the societies of those populations, which also includes production of goods, consumption of energy, and means of storing and disseminating information. Also, we have defined *complexity* as combining concepts of stratification, cultural heterogeneity, and specialization of function. We have suggested that role density varies inversely with population size and density. Now we must reconsider questions such as the following:

1. Are rural social systems necessarily of small scale?

2. Do small populations necessarily have small-scale societies?

We had better agree now on what we mean by a "small" population. Small populations studied by anthropologists have ranged from a couple of dozen people to several thousand. But not to belabor that point for the moment, let us say that ideally a small population is one of such size that the ethnographer can become acquainted with all its members during his time in the field(usually one to two years). Obviously, the definition uses the variables of both population size and duration of study. But it also implies other variables, such as the personality and energy of the ethnographer, willingness of the population to become acquainted with the ethnographer, and the like. (Almost any bull session among ethnographers produces its ethnographic horror stories, accounts ranging from hostility and ostracism to milder inaccessibility of one's informants.)

Even if we accept that definition, with all its ambiguities, other problems remain. What, for example, is meant by "become acquainted with"? That is an important question because embedded in it is the problem of which issues the ethnographer is qualified to address at the end of his fieldwork. In another sense, the question also brings us to the special kinds of ethical problems that ethnographers face.

Anthony Wallace, while developing an operational definition of personality and of culture, has devised a paradigm that is useful for thinking about the relationship between scale and complexity and what the ethnographer is qualified to discuss. He used two dimensions: number of people observed, and number of "behavior categories" observed. Each of the dimensions was subdivided, and in each cell of the resultant matrix, Wallace listed what he considered to be the proper subject of discussion for the observer at the intersection of those two conditions.[2] Now without accepting responsibility for all of Wallace's labels or his behaviorist language, we would like to use the image of such a matrix. We need not worry for the moment about how to subdivide the dimensions.

The first point that comes to mind as we think this way is that even if the lucky ethnographer should find a group of a hundred or so individuals who are willing to be "anthropologized" (using Marshall Sahlins' expression), and even if he stays long enough to get acquainted with all of them, at no time will he have observed all the things that everyone does, says, or signs through gesture or expression. To go beyond that rather trivial observation, let us take an example of a real ethnographer doing real ethnography, and see how that example

2. A. F. C. Wallace, *Culture and Personality,* 2d ed. (New York, Random House, 1970), pp. 9-18.

may be applied to the kinds of questions we have been discussing.

COMPLEXITY AND SCALE IN A NON-URBAN SOCIETY

In 1958, Anthony Leeds spent three and one-half months living with a small group of Yaruro Indians (24) in Venezuela.[3] That was long enough, and the group was small enough, for Leeds to gather detailed information about the group's subsistence activities, and somewhat less detailed information on such things as their kinship system, their religious beliefs and practices, and their form of community leadership. He was able, with such information, to suggest functional connections between those aspects of their culture (Wallace's "behavior categories" is roughly equivalent to our "aspects of culture").

Leeds made a complete survey of hunting and fishing territories and arable land, as well as tools and domesticated and wild plants and animals. Although he was not there long enough to observe a complete annual cycle, he asked people to tell him what they did in which part of the year. Also, his observations were supplemented by those of other researchers who had been present in the wet season.[4]

Contrasted with such detailed data on subsistence, Leeds' statements about religion and kinship are summary and seem to imply uniformity of beliefs and practices.[5] Although he apparently covered every adult's subsistence resources, he did not interview everyone about subsistence, cosmology or genealogies. Still his discussions of religion and kinship would fall in one cell of our matrix and his discussion of subsistence would fall in another, largely because of the greater accessibility of the subsistence data. Nevertheless, Leeds was able—we think, legitimately—to use a systemic descriptive model that included the entire community (an analytical practice that usually

ASPECTS OF CULTURE

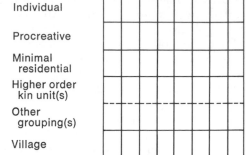

Figure 5.1
MATRIX FOR SMALL-SCALE STUDY

goes by the rather unfortunate locution "holism").

That was possible because the kind of statements he made when he descriptively tied the various aspects of culture together were at the same level of generality. Whereas he had detailed information about subsistence (or had analyzed it more thoroughly than his other data), when he discussed

3. A. Leeds, "The Ideology of the Yaruro Indians in Relation to Socio-economic Organization," *Anthropologica* 9(1960):1-10; A. Leeds, "Introduction to the Symposium," *The Evolution of Agricultural Systems in Native South America—a Symposium,* Supplemental Publication no. 2, *Anthropologica* (1961), pp. 1-12; A. Leeds, "Incipient Tropical Forest Horticulture—The Yaruro of Venezuela," *The Evolution of Agricultural Systems in Native South America—a Symposium,* Supplement publication No. 2, *Anthropologica,* Caracas, 13-46. A Leeds, "Ecological Determinants of Chieftainship among the Yaruro Indians of Venezuela," *Akten des* 34, Internationalen Amerikanistenkongress (Vienna: F. Berger, Horn, 1962), pp. 597-608.

4. V. Petrullo, "The Yaruro of the Capanaparo River, Venezuela: *Anthropological Papers,* no. 11, Bulletin 123 of the Bureau of American Ethnology.

5. In a personal communication, Leeds says that he does not think such uniformity exists. Our statement applies only to the published work.

that aspect of culture together with religion and kinship, he spoke not of the particularities, but of the general characteristics. If we decide to compare the beliefs of members of two religious cults in the United States, we may read or elicit from key informants the general doctrinal points upon which everyone purportedly agrees and compare the two at that level. If we engage in detailed conversation with each individual of one cult about his or her particular beliefs, we may still compare the two cults only in terms of general doctrine. Heterogeneity of individual beliefs within the two cults becomes a valid topic of discourse only when we have done the same detailed study of both. In a sense, then, when discussing two or more aspects of culture which fall in different cells of the matrix, we must use the lowest common denominator of particularistic information.

Now there is another lesson to be learned from Leeds' study that hits even more squarely the kind of problems one encounters in urban studies. While he was competent to make a holistic description of certain aspects of the culture of that particular group of Yaruro, he pointed out that the group itself was only a subunit of a much larger regional system. In a personal communication, Leeds says,

In Yaruro, there is the local "community" ("my village"); there are . . . a number of related villages some distance apart and in low intensity of contact; there is *"nuestra familia"*—their term—a larger group of intermarrying loosely kin-linked Yaruro with very low density of contact; and there are the *pumo*—us, in general, including kin-termed but not kin-linked Yaruro . . . on the same river. Finally there is the Kuiva-Guahibo - Yaruro - Otomaco - Piarioa - Arawakan-etc. interacting set (raid, trade, warfare, occasional intermarriage . . .). Each of these is a whole—different levels of wholes—a systemic hierarchy of wholes, with various feedback controls from level to level. . . .

From his own observations, and from those of other researchers in the area, Leeds was able to draw conclusions about the various population sets and their relationships with one another. In addition to those kinds of societal subsystems, these were also non-Indian Venezuelans, at whose hands the Yaruro suffer severe depredations, but among whom Yaruros find jobs and enter into other kinds of relationships.

Clearly, if one took the region as his or her unit of study, a new matrix, or an expansion of the old one, would be required. We can no longer duck the issue of how to subdivide the two dimensions, but here we find ourselves in a difficulty. We began, following Wallace, to speak of the number of people observed. Now, however, it is apparent that instead of numbers, we are concerned with significant groupings. For Wallace's purposes, it was sufficient to use only three subdivisions in each: "one," "two or more," and "all." For the "number of people" dimension, we would substitute a dimension composed of locally meaningful societal units, such as, perhaps, "individual," "reproductive unit," "household," "clan," and "village." This leaves the problem that there may prove to be more than one kind of unit of roughly equal scale, such as reproductive unit, and household or kinship unit. In that case, semi-partitions could be used.

For our regional matrix, it is first obvious that the units will be larger. Perhaps "village" might be the smallest. But beyond that, we have new problems. On the one hand, we may find that at the next order of inclusiveness, different units may be culturally meaningful. For example, the Yaruro have no formal multi-local organization, while other Indians in the region may have. On the other hand, we would want to index the number of each kind of subunit of each next larger unit we have studied. For example, in the case of the Yaruro's region, we have a unit called *"nuestra familia"* and the next smaller unit, "village." Then, we would

ASPECTS OF CULTURE

POPULATION UNITS	1 a b c	2 a b c	3 a b c	n a b c
Village				
Multi-local Groupings				
Region				

Figure 5.2
MATRIX FOR STUDY OF REGION

want to know how many villages of each *"nuestra familia"* had been studied.

Happily, the "aspects of culture" dimension presents fewer problems. As we have implied, we have in mind using labels for particular aspects of culture, rather than the number of such aspects. However, it should be pointed out that standardized labels such as "economy," "religion," "warfare," and the like are not necessarily meaningful in any given culture (one person's warfare being another person's economy, etc.), and care would have to be taken to devise subdivisions that made sense cross-culturally within the region studied.

SCALE AND LEVELS OF GENERALIZATION

Without working the image of the matrix to death, we should be making it obvious that a rural subject of anthropological study is not necessarily either small or culturally homogeneous, particularly if the study is regional in scope. Nor is it fanciful of us to suggest that regional studies are properly within the anthropological domain of discourse, and that such studies are of very complex systems of relations among very

different kinds of units. Scholars such as Julian Steward and Eric Wolf have been calling for systemic regional and national studies since the mid-1950s. The response to this call, unfortunately, did not come quickly. However, in the past five years a number of excellent regional studies have been undertaken, and the need for that kind of study is generally recognized.

As we have implied, the issue of whether or not rural populations must have small-scale societies pivots on one's level of generalization; but even at that, it remains a question to be answered with empirical evidence. Degree of cultural homogeneity may also vary from one aspect of culture to another. In a peasant village in Mexico, for example, Uzzell found considerable uniformity in many aspects of the local subculture, but rather pronounced variation of illness beliefs.[6] Similarly, in a regional study one may find considerable diversity among villages or among systems of villages.

At the level of the village, the Yaruro appear to have a noncomplex society. There is little or no vertical stratification, no institutionalized government. Also, one would expect high role density. We do not mean for our rule of thumb about role density and size and density of population to be taken as a rigid law. In fact, it is conceivable that in some cases complex organization might promote high role density.

Role density is a notion perhaps best explained in terms of social networks. The concept of social networks is complicated by variable terminology as well as by theoretical differences. After introducing the concept here in the most general terms, we shall devote somewhat more space to it in chapter 7.

Imagine a net, like a fishing net. Now, let each intersection of the string represent

---

6. D. Uzzell, "*Susto* Revisited: Illness as Strategic Role," *American Ethnologist* 1(1974):369-78.

a person, and each connecting string represent a relationship between two people in a population. If a fishing net stood for a social field, each person would have one kind of relationship with each of four other people. On the one hand, we have this master network of an entire population or a socially significant subset. We may also speak of ego-centered networks (all the people with relations with a particular person) or non-ego-centered networks that represent parts of the larger network.

Now a fishing net is far too simple to make a good representation of a social network.[7] One person may have more than one kind of relationship with another person (as diagrammed in figure 1, chapter 4); a variety of kinds of relationships, each with a different person; or some combination of the two. A social role may be thought of as an identity of one person that in some way determines his or her relationship with one or more other people. Each role implies a reciprocal role in the second person in the relationship.

Role density, then, refers to the average number of links (relationships) per dyad in a social network, each kind of dyadic relationship, as we have said, implying a pair of roles. Networks of sets of a population may very well have different role densities, as has been shown by a series of studies by Willmott and Young, Townsend, and Bott in London.[8] The picture there is that residents of the East London slums, living close to kinsmen and former schoolmates and maintaining multi-stranded relationships with those people, exhibit higher role density than members of the so-called middle class.

One aspect of low role density, coupled with a high inventory of possible roles—usually associated with urban settings—is that because one is constantly establishing single-strand relationships with unknown or relatively unknown people, there is maxi-

mum opportunity to negotiate roles, rather than having them ascribed by the community. That this is a strictly urban phenomenon, however, is doubtful, simply because not all small populations have homogeneous cultures. Edmund Leach describes a Kachin community of five hundred which he feels to be homogeneous even though in 1940 it included subgroups speaking Jinghpaw, Gauri, Asi, Maru, Lisu, and Chinese.[9] Whether or not this community is culturally homogeneous, language carries with it sub-ethnic identity that may or may not limit the number of roles possible to an individual actor. Provencher describes a situation in a Malaysian community in which not only do individuals negotiate roles within their sub-ethnic groups, but also, he says,

Most adults are aware of, and can often perform, the customs of other sub-ethnic groups. Many can speak at least one dialect other than their own and can caricature several others. A single individual may claim several sub-ethnic identities, each in its appropriate situation, through his ability to perform their character-

7. There is a danger, when one is dealing with this or any other analytical concept, of becoming confused about its ontological status. Networks, systems, cultures, roles, and the like are mythical entities invented by the analyst to help him or her explain some part of the world. They do not function at the level of human actors, except possibly to the extent that the actors also use them to interpret the world and in doing so are influenced in their decision making.

8. E. Bott, *Family and Social Network: Roles Norms, and External Relations in Ordinary Urban Families* (London: Tavistock, 1957); P. Wilmott and M. Young, *Family and Class in a London Suburb* (London: Routledge and Kegan Paul, 1960); M. Young and P. Wilmott, *Family & Kinship in East London* (London: Routledge and Kegan Paul, 1957).

9. E. R. Leach, *Political Systems of Highland Burma* (Boston: Beacon Press, 1965—first published 1954).

istic behavior and through a claim of affinal or distant consanguineal relationship.[10]

Returning to the region where the Yaruro live, while it is clearly socially and culturally heterogeneous, the Indian part of it is not stratified. But the non-Indian population is structurally part of the complex Venezuelan state. Within any given segment role density remains high.

At the other extreme, Benedict cites large segmentary tribal groups such as the Tiv of Nigeria, perhaps a million strong.[11] Despite their number, Tiv society consists of a repetition of a simple organizational principle.[12] This is a case of a large population with a noncomplex society, and presumably, within segments, high role density.

Complex social organization may also contribute to high role density by isolating societal strata and enforcing limited population and availability of roles within each stratum. It would appear that this may have been the case in the Ankole state, which, though complicated (not complex) at the level of the court, and complex at the state level, appears to have resembled the Tiv in its local groups.

CONCLUSION

There remain the problems of data that are representative and analyses that have implications for general social theory. We have already dealt with those problems in the first part of the chapter. However, it seems appropriate to point out one additional consideration here. The major precaution that the anthropologist who does not use statistical measures of reliability must take in urban places is the same as one that he or she must take in rural places: to ask constantly, "How do I know this?" and "How sure am I that this statement will stand in every case?" and to make his or her reservations clear in reports. That means that most statements will be equivocal.

What we often forget is that *all* statements of statistical significance are equivocal. But usually, statistical statements fall at the end of a chain of assumptions in which data are interpreted in ways that are subject to other interpretations. The effect of statistical statements of reliability is that they mask the very high degree of equivocation that lie behind them and give a spurious sense of precision, concreteness, and general "scientific" rigor.

So as we move to the study of urban places, the two hobgoblins that are supposed to bedevil anthropologists when they move to urban places—social scale and cultural heterogeneity—may indeed be frightful; but they are old acquaintances.

For Further Reading

Banton, M., ed. *The Anthropology of Complex Societies*, A.S.A. Monograph number 4 (London: Tavistock Publications, 1966). Several very basic articles.

Bibliography

Leach, E. R. 1965—first published 1954. *Political Systems of Highland Burma*. Boston: Beacon Press.

10. R. Provencher, *Two Malay Worlds: Interaction in Urban and Rural Settings*, Research Monograph no. 4, Center for South and Southeast Asia Studies, University of California, Berkeley (Berkeley and Los Angeles: University of California Press, 1971), pp. 99-100.

11. B. Benedict, "Sociological Characteristics of Small Territories and their Implications for Economic Development," in *The Social Anthropology of Complex Societies*, A.S.A. Monograph no. 4, ed. M. Banton (London: Tavistock, 1966).

12. Ibid., p. 24. *See also*, P. Bohannan, *Justice and Judgment Among the Tiv* (London: Oxford University Press, 1957); M. D. Sahlins, "The Segmentary Lineage: An Organization of Predatory Expansion," *American Anthropologist* 63(1961): 322-45.

Leeds, A. 1969. "The Significant Variables Determining the Character of Squatter Settlements." *America Latina* 12:44-86.

Plotnicov, L. 1973. "Anthropological Field Work in Modern and Local Urban Contexts." *Urban Anthropology* 2:248-64.

Weaver, T. and White, D. 1972. "Anthropological Approaches to Urban and Complex Society." *The Anthropology of Urban Environments*, Society for Applied Anthropology Monograph Series, Monograph number 11, edited by T. Weaver and D. White. Boulder: Society for Applied Anthropology.

6 | Recent Studies of Urban Life

If rural populations have cultures or subcultures that are different from those of urban populations, then the movement of rural people into urban places should entail some kind of culture change, both for the receiving populations and for the incoming populations. Studies of the adaptation of rural-urban migrants, then, are squarely within a traditional anthropological field of inquiry into cultural change and acculturation. One factor that has made studies of urban adaptation problematic, however, is the forcefulness of Western folk beliefs in shaping professional views of the nature of rural (and urban) culture.

THE FOLK-URBAN CONTINUUM

The anthropologist who is most frequently singled out for criticism in this regard is Robert Redfield. But it might well be argued that Redfield's major "sin," compared with the work of many of his contemporaries, was success. Far too many ethnographies written during the first half of this century are cloyingly replete with assertions of the sweetness and light of rural culture. Redfield stated the myth in larger theoretical terms than most, and his formulation was taken up eagerly by anthropologists and sociologists alike. It was the same myth

that we referred to in chapter 4 as Rousseauean romantic rural society (RRRS), and in Redfield's case it was at least partly shaped by the early Chicago sociologists, who were his professors, colleagues, and in-laws.

While the Chicago sociologists were busily mapping the "problems" of urban life, Redfield went off to Mexico to study a peasant village not far from Mexico City. His study of Tepoztlan was published in 1930.[1] That study, coupled with further work in Yucatan, led him to formulate the notion of a continuum from "folk culture" to "urban culture." The folk pole was an RRRS, and the urban pole was essentially the image expressed (later, though formulated earlier) in Wirth's "Urbanism as a Way of Life."[2]

Redfield's ideal type of folk community, which he points out may never correspond to a real culture, is "small, isolated, nonliterate, and homogeneous, with a strong sense of group solidarity." He adds that

1. R. Redfield, *Tepoztlan: A Mexican Village* (Chicago: University of Chicago Press, 1930).

2. L. Wirth, "Urbanism as a Way of Life," *American Journal of Sociology* 44(1938):1-24; R. Redfield, "Culture Changes in Yucatan," *American Anthropologist* 36(1934):57-69; R. Redfield, *The Folk Culture of Yucatan* (Chicago: University of Chicago Press, 1941).

there is no legislation or habit of experiment and reflection for intellectual ends. Kinship, its relationships and institutions, are the type categories of experience and the familial group is the unit of action. The sacred prevails over the secular; the economy is one of status rather than of the market.[3]

Originally, Redfield considered the independent variables in this list to be isolation and cultural homogeneity, with other variables in the list dependent. Later, however, after Sol Tax showed that physically isolated, culturally homogeneous communities in Guatemala exhibited many of the putatively urban characteristics,[4] Redfield suggested that there might be other sufficient causes—in the Guatemalan case, a market economy. Of course, once such a possibility is admitted, the continuum no longer goes from rural to urban.

For Redfield, the position of any given locality along the continuum is not fixed. Rather, cultural change is seen as radiating from urban center to hinterland, with progressive urbanization resulting. A great many criticisms eventually came to be leveled at the construct, some based on logic, others based on field research. Kroeber, for example, found the logical extreme of the "urban culture" type—which would be absolutely atomistic, secular, formal, non-familial, and impersonal—impossible to imagine.[5] It was pointed out by some that large population segments, such as rural proletariats, were left out of the scheme entirely; others demonstrated that many rural communities fail to exhibit a great number of the purportedly "folk" characteristics. The formulation became so controversial during the late 1940s and early 1950s that, as Richard Adams has remarked, "Sol Tax, then editor of the *American Anthropologist*, announced . . . that he simply would not accept any more articles on the subject."[6]

One of Redfield's major detractors was Oscar Lewis, who, like Redfield, attracted a great deal of attention outside as well as within the discipline. We shall discuss Lewis here because of the prominence of his "culture-of-poverty" formulation and the extensiveness of his rebuttal against Redfield's folk-urban continuum. We want, though, to avoid the easy rhetorical device of hanging the issues on a series of personalistic coathooks. We are dealing with ideas, not dynasties.

The first stage of Lewis' attack on the folk-urban continuum began with a restudy of Tepoztlan, twenty years after Redfield had worked there. Using a large staff of researchers and a variety of techniques, Lewis compiled a much more impressive body of data than Redfield, working alone, had done. Based on that information, Lewis concluded that Tepoztlan was at best a poor representative of the folk end of the continuum. About the formulation in general, he argued (1) that it focuses attention unnecessarily on cities as the source of cultural change, (2) that changes in cultural heterogeneity may stem from other causes than urbanism, (3) that the definition of folk culture obscures differences among rural communities, (4) that the formulation is a poor guide for research because of the narrowness of its focus, (5) that there are no compelling reasons for assuming a causal relationship between the various elements, and (6) that the whole scheme is shot through

3. R. Redfield, "The Folk Society," *American Journal of Sociology* 52(January 1947):294.

4. S. Tax, "World View and Social Relations in Guatemala," *American Anthropologist* 43(January-March 1941):27-42.

5. A. L. Kroeber, *Anthropology* (New York: Harcourt, Brace and Co., 1948), pp. 280-86.

6. R. N. Adams, "Introduction," in *Contemporary Cultures and Societies of Latin America*, ed. D. B. Heath and R. N. Adams (New York: Random House, 1965), p. 7.

with value judgments in which folk equals good and urban equals bad.[7]

Next, Lewis traced Tepoztecan migrants to Mexico City, and based on research among them, concluded that institutions such as the family, fictive kinship, and religion, though modified, were altogether strengthened in the urban milieu, not destroyed as Redfield's formulation would have led one to expect.[8]

Though it would appear that nobody takes the folk-urban continuum very seriously anymore, we should not forget that Redfield forthrightly posed a question that has been posed by other thinkers such as Tönnies and Durkheim: Is there a qualitative difference between culture in urban places and culture in rural places that is universal and that is caused by some characteristic of urbanness? Few of Redfield's detractors confronted that question in its broadest sense, and it remains unanswered.

Horace Miner sought to test the generality of Redfield's model, assuming that it was an accurate description of Western urban places, and wishing to see if it held good for non-Western urban places as well. Miner's study of Timbuctoo was inconclusive, although Miner himself claimed that it supported Redfield. On the one hand, indices of social disorganization that Miner used, such as divorce rate, are ethnocentric and tell us little about the local culture. On the other hand, incidental data in Miner's report seem to indicate homogeneity, religiosity, strong family ties, and the like within ethnic subcultures, with the putatively urban characteristics occurring only between members of different subcultures.[9]

THE CULTURE-OF-POVERTY

On the surface, Oscar Lewis' later work implies a negative answer to the question Redfield was treating—and an alternative hypothesis. However, he maintains many of the old prejudices against urban life-styles.

It is not, Lewis argues, the demographic aspects of urbanism that create the "undesirable" elements of urban cultures and subcultures, but poverty. (Although Lewis maintains that a culture-of- poverty may be found in rural as well as in urban localities, all his culture-of-poverty studies were conducted in urban places.)

It is a little difficult to pin down Lewis' theoretical construct because it is scattered over the introductions of various books and several articles, beginning with the 1959 publication of *Five Families,* in the subtitle of which the term is coined.[10] Most of these are popular works in which rigor and thoroughness probably would have been inappropriate. Moreover, the idea seems to take shape gradually over the years, and there is no lack of contradictions between publications (and even within some). Finally, Lewis has been interpreted and his ideas simplified, expanded, and distorted so extensively that it is hard to remember what Lewis himself said.

Nevertheless, we may generalize that the culture-of-poverty was seen by Lewis as a pattern of attitudes and behavior characterized by personal and social disorganization and disaffiliation from the larger society. Although that pattern supposedly grows out of the process of adapting to the situation of being poor, it is not to be construed as the only possible adaptation: Lewis distin-

7. O. Lewis, *Life in a Mexican Village: Tepoztlan Restudied* (Urbana: University of Illinois Press, 1951).

8. O. Lewis, "Urbanization Without Breakdown," *The Scientific Monthly* 75(1952):31-41.

9. H. Miner, "The Folk-Urban Continuum," *American Sociological Review* 17(October 1952): 529-37.

10. O. Lewis, *Five Families: Mexican Case Studies in the Culture of Poverty* (New York: Basic Books, 1959). Perhaps the most systematic statement is to be found in O. Lewis, "The Culture of Poverty," *Scientific American* 215(1966):19-25.

guishes between poverty and the culture-of-poverty.

So far, this is no advance over the Chicago sociologists, but Lewis goes a critical step further by "scientizing" yet another folk belief, one which goes back at least to the Calvinist doctrine that financial success is indicative of divine favor, and as a corollary to that, the poor either are actively to blame for their poverty, or are inferior. In Lewis' hands, that myth is restated as follows: once in existence, the culture-of-poverty prevents economic success by fostering inappropriate attitudes and behavior; at the same time, it perpetuates itself by similarly enculturating successive generations.

Lewis' chief technique for gathering and presenting data was to interview members of selected poor families (mostly in Mexico City, San Juan, Puerto Rico, and New York) in his home or office, thereby eliciting autobiographical sketches, some of which he edited and published. These were supplemented by descriptions of the neighborhoods where the families lived. Unfortunately, Lewis tells us little about how he selected families or how he chose particular excerpts from their autobiographies. In fact, anyone familiar with the urban poor, particularly those of us who have been poor ourselves, must suspect that he may have chosen deviant extremes, rather than typical populations. Even so, the words of Lewis' informants often contradict his formulations.

Considering the theoretical and methodological weakness of Lewis' later work, it is surprising that it attracted the attention of anthropologists at all. But attract attention it did. In the late 1960s no meeting of anthropologists was complete without its group of papers on the culture-of-poverty—mostly critical. The explanation of this curious phenomenon lies largely outside the discipline.

First of all, Lewis sought and received a wide popular audience. Second, he began publishing his culture-of-poverty ideas at the beginning of a decade that was to see a great deal of agitation from poor people in the United States. Third, by cloaking old class and ethnic prejudices in pseudoscientific language, he appealed to a large number of politicians, bureaucrats, academics, and popular social philosophers who found his doctrine timely and congenial. Charles Valentine, one of Lewis' major detractors, says,

The cult [of followers of the culture-of-poverty formulation] enables the affluent to take a benevolent stance toward the dispossessed without granting them any respect. The doctrine confirms the social inferiority of those who live in poverty. It lets social superiors feel they can be patrons of the poor without losing much. It articulates well with cliches of the political center like "opportunity" and "equality," but it arouses little anxiety that these slogans will be taken literally by anyone in power. . . . The official attitudes, manners, and values of the middle class are assiduously inculcated to combat the "culture" of the poor that is said to be holding them back. If all this does little to change inadequate subsistence, unemployment, exploitation, political powerlessness, police oppression, and the many other hard realities of poverty, the underlying doctrine has not really been violated.[11]

A full critique of the culture-of-poverty would take more than one volume, and indeed, it has already been done.[12] Among

11. C. A. Valentine, "The 'Culture of Poverty': Its Scientific Significance and Its Implications for Action," in The Culture of Poverty: A Critique, ed. E. B. Leacock (New York: Simon & Schuster, 1971), p. 217.
12. See E. B. Leacock, ed., The Culture of Poverty: A Critique (New York: Simon & Schuster, 1971), particularly Leacock's introduction and the articles by Leeds and Valentine. Also, see C. A. Valentine, Culture and Poverty: Critique and Counter-Proposals (Chicago: University of Chicago Press, 1968).

most anthropologists, it is a dead issue. The only reason we have devoted as much space to it as we have is that the concept is still alive and well in some areas and is likely to be encountered in one form or another by any student of urban life. For example, in 1970, Uzzell gave a briefing to officials of the United States Agency for International Development in Lima, Peru. The briefing dealt with squatter settlements in and around Lima, and it ended with a description of the organizations in these localities, such as householders' associations, women's clubs, youth clubs, parent-teacher organizations, sports clubs, and ad hoc committees for the accomplishment of various self-help projects. One bemused official said after the briefing, "Yes, that's all well and good, but can you tell us how to help these people organize their society and give their lives some order and meaning?"

SOCIAL STRUCTURE

Redfield's formulation dealt mainly with hypothetical urban and rural life-styles, with a unitary treatment of urban culture. Lewis' later work focused on life-styles of some impoverished urbanites, to the exclusion of other urban populations. Neither attempted to treat the total social structures of urban places or regions. Perhaps the earliest, and surely the best known, anthropological study of social structure was done by Lloyd Warner. The social structure that Warner and his associates saw in Yankee City (Newburyport, Massachusetts) has become the familiar three-class model that most American social scientists use, with the difference that Warner's original concept which focused on institutions and interaction, has been replaced with a statistical approach using factors such as occupation and education for placing people in classes.[13] And to the extent that it competes with Marxist and neo-Marxist models, it

carries with it a certain amount of ideological and political freight.

Although a great many anthropologists have concerned themselves with social stratification of urban places, regions, and nations, the only systematic comparison of social structure in two cities was undertaken in Mexico and Columbia by Whiteford in the late 1950s.[14] Nevertheless, a growing number of anthropologists question the universality of both the Warnerian and the Marxist models of class structures, and alternative criteria for ranking populations hierarchically have been proposed. Walter Goldschmidt has suggested that six bases have been used to identify classes:

1. Defined classes: such as the castes of India.
2. Cultural classes: populations with obvious subcultures.
3. Economic classes: populations with distinctive relationships to the means of production.
4. Political classes: populations with differing degrees of power or authority.
5. Self-identified classes.
6. Participation classes: populations with differential access to certain kinds of interaction.[15]

13. *See* W. L. Warner and P. S. Lunt, *The Social Life of a Modern Community* (New Haven: Yale University Press, 1941).

14. *See* J. H. Steward, et al., *The People of Puerto Rico* (Urbana: University of Illinois Press, 1956); N. E. Whitten, Jr., *Class, Kinship, and Power in an Ecuadorian Town: The Negroes of San Lorenzo* (Stanford: Stanford University Press, 1965); E. A. Hammel, *Wealth, Authority and Prestige in the Ica Valley, Peru,* University of New Mexico Publications in Anthropology, no. 10 (Albuquerque: University of New Mexico Press, 1962); A. H. Whiteford, *Two Cities of Latin America: A Comparative Description of Social Classes,* Logan Museum Publications in Anthropology, no. 9 (Beloit, Wisc.: Beloit College, 1960).

15. Cited in R. L. Beals, "Social Stratification in Latin America," *American Journal of Sociology* 58(1953):327-39.

More is involved, however, than just hitting upon suitable criteria. Unresolved in most of the literature is the very ontological status of "classes." Also unclear is the utility of analytically defining classes where such definitions do not account for cultural phenomena. Finally, in most complex societies, hierarchical strata are segmented and the segments themselves may cut across strata.[16] Nor does a mere ranking of members of a population necessarily tell us anything about the mechanisms by which societal units are articulated with each other. Indeed, Eric Wolf has suggested that a major focus of anthropologists should be precisely upon those individuals and institutions that mediate between social units.[17]

If urban cultures are seen as systems, no description of any single element can be complete until other relevant elements and their mutual relationships are defined. Clearly, a standard model for analyzing social structure is required if we are to make useful comparisons of the cultural systems of urban places and regions. Development of such a model is still in the future. Meanwhile, we doubt that the statistical approach of placing people in social categories on the basis of a handful of traits will prove very useful until *after* such a general model is developed. To do so now, when we still do not know what the meaningful categories might be, is only a waste of time and a practice that serves only to hide our ignorance from ourselves and the public.

URBANIZATION AND ADAPTATION

Most studies by U. S. anthropologists in urban places have dealt with rural-urban migrants, bounded localities, or distinctive population sets that may or may not be geographically bonded (including migrants). In the United States, itself, a number of studies have been directed at Indian-Americans.[18] Studies elsewhere in the world have been dominated by an interest in rural-ur-

ban migrants—so much so that one of the first urban anthropology anthologies to be published in the United States was entitled *Peasants in Cities* (although not all the migrants discussed therein were former peasants and not all the contributors were anthropologists).[19]

AFRICAN STUDIES

Studies by British social anthropologists and sociologists in sub-Saharan Africa are of special interest—first because urban studies were being conducted fairly widely there at least a decade earlier than elsewhere (a fact partly attributable to the greater affinity between sociology and social anthropology in England than in the United States, and, second, because of some of the peculiarities of many urban places in Africa. Most African towns and cities south of the Sahara have been created only recently and for colonial purposes. That is to say, they have not evolved from indigenous societies. Even the older nonindustrial towns and cities have had their economic bases changed radically. Further, in the British colonies, particularly, the African populations of the newly created urban places often were stringently controlled in ways that shaped the demographic and ecological pat-

16. A. Leeds, "Some Problems in the Analysis of Class and the Social Order," *Social Structure, Stratification, and Mobility* (Washington D.C.: Pan American Union, General Secretariat of the Organization of American States, 1967).

17. *See* E. R. Wolf, "Kinship, Friendship, and Patron-Client Relations in Complex Societies," in *The Social Anthropology of Complex Societies*, A. S. A. Monographs number 4, ed. M. Banton (London: Tavistock Publications, 1966), pp. 1-20.

18. Such studies have been collected in J. O. Waddell and O. M. Watson, eds., *The American Indian in Urban Society* (Boston: Little, Brown & Co., 1971).

19. W. Mangin, ed., *Peasants in Cities: Readings in the Anthropology of Urbanization* (Boston: Houghton Mifflin Co., 1970).

terns of the settlements. J. Clyde Mitchell (a sociologist) lists six "external imperatives" common to such urban places, noting that some of the imperatives probably are common to all urban places.

1. Population density.

2. Mobility: This is not just the greater than natural increase of urban populations or the residential mobility normally associated with urban life-styles, but also a movement back and forth from rural to urban places and circulation among towns. In some places, mine owners and other European employers forbade or discouraged permanent residence in the towns, and by not providing for the welfare of workers in their old age or disability, effectively forced employees to maintain contacts with their places of origin.

3. Heterogeneity: In Africa this takes the form of population segments with distinctive tribal membership, as well as the presence of considerable non-African populations.

4. Economic differentiations.

5. Demographic disproportion: A disproportionate number of young male manual laborers are found in most cities.

6. Administrative and political limitations: Besides the effects noted in items 2 and 5, such limitations also affect relations among Africans and between Africans and non-Africans.[20]

In Africa, as elsewhere, anthropologists have shown a great deal of interest in urbanization and the adaptation of rural migrants to urban places. Perhaps because of their familiarity with rural cultures (often of tribally organized populations in Africa), many researchers have attempted to understand subcultures in urban places as built from the components of rural cultures. This point of view, however, has been questioned by Southall, Mayer, Mitchell, and others, who point out that individuals, not cultures, migrate.[21] Migrants behave according to the dictates of situations within which they must follow distinctive sets of rules. Thus, according to that view, rural-urban migrants become bicultural, much as one becomes bilingual.

With that rationale in mind, Mitchell has called for "situational analyses" of urban life that take into account the constraints within which the individual operates, rather than historical analyses, which invoke elements of rural culture. It is interesting that Radcliffe-Brown, perhaps the most influential British anthropologist of this century, was making the same kind of plea, though not for urban studies, over fifty years ago.

SITUATIONAL ANALYSES IN THE UNITED STATES

If by "situational analyses" we are to understand analysis that takes cognizance of contextual factors impinging on the norms, values, and behavior of populations studied, then we may say that situational analysis has characterized some of the best urban studies done in the United States and elsewhere in recent years. Two examples come immediately to mind: Elliot Liebow's ethnography of men in Washington, D.C., who spend a great deal of their time on street corners,[22] and James Spradley's study of al-

20. J. C. Mitchell, "Theoretical Orientations in African Urban Studies," in *The Social Anthropology of Complex Societies*, A.S.A. Monographs number 4, ed. M. Banton (London: Tavistock Publications, 1966), pp. 48-50.

21. P. Mayer, *Townsmen or Tribesmen: Conservatism and the Process of Urbanization in a South African City* (Cape Town: Oxford University Press, 1961); P. Mayer, "Migrancy and the Study of Africans in Town," *American Anthropologist* 64(1962)576-92; A. Southall, "Introductory Summary," in *Social Change in Modern Africa*, ed. A. Southall (London: Oxford University Press, 1961), pp. 1-46; J. C. Mitchell, ibid.

22. E. Liebow, *Tally's Corner: A Study of Negro Streetcorner Men* (Boston: Little, Brown & Co., 1967).

coholic urban nomads, especially in Seattle.[23]

In both of these studies, extensive participant observation and interviewing led the ethnographers to understand their informants' views of the world well enough to perceive an order and reasonableness that is invisible to outsiders. That is almost always the case with successful ethnography. The fact that both Spradley and Liebow looked not only deeply within the subcultures they were studying, but also outside to the structure of interaction between those populations and elements of the larger society is what makes both studies outstanding. Both show that what is considered deviant behavior by outsiders is amplified, if not partially caused, by the nature of the population's outside interactions. In Spradley's case, the study has actually led to changes in Seattle's laws for treating alcoholic tramps.

It is the quality of discovering relevant structural constraints that sets off these studies from mere descriptions.[24] Such studies are also the corrective for superficial ethnocentric formulations such as the culture-of-poverty. An increasing number of social scientists now at least pay lip service to the idea that deviance is culturally determined, because what is normative in a given culture is seldom universally normative, and deviance is, as it were, the reciprocal of normativeness. But what is seldom understood is (1) that what is deviant in the larger culture, or in dominant subcultures, may be normative in other subcultures, (2) how this may be so, and (3) how the structure may reinforce the very behavior it condemns.

This is not mere social determinism. Obviously, not everybody becomes an alcoholic urban nomad; not all black males organize a major part of their lives around a street corner. Much remains to be learned about the processes by which members of these and other populations come to be members. But the two studies mentioned are beginnings. They show how, once one has become a member, membership is maintained and lives are structured. And most importantly, they view the world through nonethnocentric lenses.

IRREGULAR SETTLEMENTS

In much of the so-called third world, the high rate of rural-urban migration, coupled with the low incomes of most migrants, has created such a severe housing shortage that where public or private land is available around cities, it is often occupied by people needing housing, and the construction of houses is begun. Means of occupying the land are extremely varied, but the one characteristic common to all irregular settlements is that usufruct of the land is obtained in some manner other than the way that the commercial housing industry normally operates. Sometimes land is illegally invaded, police pressure is resisted, and residents simply occupy their house sites by force and by squatters' rights. Hence, the name "squatter settlements" is often used. In other cases, however, settlement is overtly or covertly encouraged by the public or private owners for their own ends; and in some places, residents actually purchase the land one way or another. Thus, we feel that the term "irregular settlements" is preferable to the term "squatter settlements."

A number of anthropologists have been attracted to the study of irregular settlements because of their visibility, because they usually contain a high proportion of

23. J. P. Spradley, *You Owe Yourself a Drunk: An Ethnography of Urban Nomads* (Boston: Little, Brown & Co., 1970).

24. Such descriptions, while probably preferable to more surveys, tend to leave one with a distinct feeling of frustration. One quarterly journal, *Urban Life and Culture,* seems to be devoted primarily to that kind of treatment of urban phenomena.

formerly rural people, and because their existence is often considered by local authorities to constitute a social, economic, health, or aesthetic "problem." The perceived severity of the "problem" varies from country to country. Whereas in Brazil, *favelas*, as they are called, are considered "cancers on the face" of Rio de Janiero to be surgically removed if such were possible, in Peru, irregular settlement has become virtually the backbone of national urban planning,[25]

In irregular settlements, as elsewhere, participant observation usually gives the lie to popular myths of the horrors of such neighborhoods. In some cases, perhaps spurred by nonacademic considerations, there is a tendency to overreact, so that irregular settlement and self-built housing are spoken of in Panglossian terms as the best of all possible solutions to local housing shortages.[26] Of course such treatments overlook the fact that the shortage exists in the first place partly because of the unequal distribution of capital. That is, while such arguments may reflect points of view from the inside, they are inadequate contextually.

Basically, there are two approaches to the study of irregular settlements. The first focuses on the residents as one or another kind of urban population. Such studies usually run up against the fact that only a portion of the life of the dweller in an irregular settlement takes place in the settlement itself.[27] The second, which concerns itself with the development of the locality, per se, might as well be conducted in any other locality in the urban place.[28] None of this is to say that studies of irregular settlements are inappropriate for urban anthropologists, but that the attention given them probably has been disproportionate.

RECENTLY PUBLISHED STUDIES

A quick review of themes and issues can communicate the variety of questions posed

and techniques used for answering them by anthropologists now studying in urban places. With that in mind, we have selected twenty-four articles, published recently in anthropological journals and anthologies, to present in the remainder of this chapter.[29] Because of the time lag between research and publication, most of the research reported in the articles was conducted in the 1960s. Our selection is intended to represent

25. A. Leeds, "Brazil and the Myth of Urban Rurality: Urban Experience and Want in Squatments in Rio de Janeiro and Lima," in *City and Country in the Third World*, ed. A. J. Field (Cambridge: Schenkman, 1969).

26. *See* J. Turner, "Barriers and Channels for Housing Development in Westernizing Countries," in *Peasants in Cities: Readings in the Anthropology of Urbanization*, ed. W. Mangin (Boston: Houghton Mifflin Co., 1970), pp. 1-19; W. Mangin, "Latin American Squatter Settlements: A Problem and a Solution," in *Latin American Research Review* 2(3)(Summer 1967):94-127.

27. B. Roberts, *Organizing Strangers: The Careers and Politics of Poor Families in Guatemala City* (Austin: University of Texas Press, in press).

28. *See* for example, A. Leeds, "The Significant Variables Determining the Character of Squatter Settlements," *America Latino* 12(3)(1969):44-86; D. Uzzell, "The Interaction of Population and Locality in the Development of Squatter Settlements in Lima," in *Latin American Urban Research*, vol. 4, ed. W. Cornelius and F. Trueblood.

29. Four sources were used: Two issues of *Urban Anthropology*; one issue of *American Ethnologist*; an anthology edited by T. Weaver and D. White, entitled *The Anthropology of Urban Environments*; and an anthology edited by G. M. Foster and R. V. Kemper, entitled *Anthropologists in Cities*. The articles from each are as follows:

From G. M. Foster and R. V. Kemper, eds., *Anthropologists in Cities* (Boston: Little, Brown & Co., 1974). M. Whiteford, "Barrio Tulcan: Fieldwork in a Columbia City," pp. 41-62.

From *American Ethnologist* 1(1)(1974). T. D. Graves, "Urban Indian Personality and the Culture of Poverty," pp. 65-86; M. Micklin, M. Durbin and C. A. Leon, "The Lexicon for Madness in a Columbian City: An Exploration of Semantic Space," pp. 143-56.

From *Urban Anthropology* 2(2)(Fall 1973). S. Barnett, "Urban Is as Urban Does: Two Incidents

roughly the most current literature on anthropological studies in urban places (although we suspect that one or two of the authors are not anthropologists). It was not our intention to present only the best papers. Indeed, we deem some of the articles to be poor, and many excellent articles were not selected.

ADAPTATION OF MIGRANTS

Predictably, the biggest number of studies in our sample (eight) are concerned with the adaptation of migrants to urban places. Three of the reports discuss migrants in both rural and urban settings. Simic and Ferraro focus on kinship. Simic examines the maintenance of ties between urban migrants and their rural kinsmen in Serbia and sees this as responsible for the smoothness of peasant adaptation to urban life. Ferraro samples recent and older migrants in Nairobi and a rural population to test Southall's hypothesis that urban roles are more narrowly defined than rural ones. Interestingly, he finds little difference between rural and old-time urban role definitions, but some difference between those two and the urban newcomers.

Working in Port Moresby, the Salisburys, like Simic, treat urban center and hinterland as a single social system. However, they are more interested in economic decision making within a social context. Their work is one of the few attempts at a close analysis of the decision processes that lead to migration. Unfortunately, in the absence of such studies, "explanations" of migration have been left largely to economists, whose models (often little more than slogans) have been too general to be of much value. The Salisbury study is interesting, also, because it treats return migration, which for the Siane is often a desirable strategy. This contrasts with the situation in Jos, Nigeria, in which, according to Plotnicov, migrants are virtually trapped in the cities by a set of

expectations of themselves and their rural kin that very few of them can meet.[30]

Doughty, Fleuret, and Hirabayashi and his colleagues all look at institutional mech-

---

on One Street in Madras City, South India," pp. 129-60; V. R. Dorjahn, "Some Rural-Urban Marriage Differentials: The Temne of Magburaka Town and Its Environs," pp. 161-81; G. P. Ferraro, "Tradition or Transition?: Rural and Urban Kinsmen in East Africa," pp. 214-31; L. Plotnicov, "Anthropological Field Work Modern and Local Urban Contexts," pp. 248-64; I. Press, "Bureaucracy vs. Folk Medicine: Implications from Seville, Spain," pp. 232-47; E. S. Segal, "Ethnic Variables in East African Urban Migration," pp. 194-204; A. Simic, "Kinship Reciprocity and Rural-Urban Integration in Serbia," pp. 205-13.

From *Urban Anthropology* 3(1)(Spring, 1974). A. K. Fleuret, "Incorporation into Networks—Among Sikhs in Los Angeles," pp. 27-46; M. J. Mochon, "Working Class Constraints and Choices: An Urban Case Study," pp. 47-63; J. A. Nagata, "Tale of Two Cities: The Role of Non-Urban Factors in Community Life in Two Malaysian Towns," pp. 1-26; R. W. Thompson, "Rural-Urban Differences in Individual Modernization in Buganda," pp. 64-78; D. Uzzell, "A Strategic Analysis of Social Structure in Lima, Peru, Using the Concept of 'Plays,'" pp. 34-46.

From T. Weaver and D. White, eds., *The Anthropology of Urban Environments* Monograph number 11; (Boulder: The Society for Applied Anthropology, 1972), P. L. Doughty, "Peruvian Migrant Identity in the Urban Milieu," pp. 39-50; D. G. Epstein, "The Genesis and Function of Squatter Settlements in Brasilia," pp. 51-58; H. G. Nutini, "The Latin American City: A Cultural-Historical Approach," pp. 89-96; P. J. Pelto, "Research Strategies in the Study of Complex Societies: The 'Ciudad-Industrial Project,'" pp. 5-20; R. Provencher, "Comparisons of Social Interaction Styles: Urban and Rural Malay Culture," pp. 69-76; R. E. Salisbury and M. Salisbury, "The Rural-Oriented Strategy of Urban Adaptation: Siane Migrants in Port Moresby," pp. 59-68; J. Hirabayashi, W. Willard, and L. Kemnitzer, "Pan-Indianism in the Urban Setting," pp. 77-88; J. P. Spradley, "Adaptive Strategies of Urban Nomads: The Ethnoscience of Tramp Culture," pp. 21-38.

30. L. Plotnicov, "Nigerians: The Dream is Unfulfilled," in *Peasants in Cities: Readings in the Anthropology of Urbanization*, ed. W. Mangin (Boston: Houghton Mifflin Co., 1970).

anisms of adaptation. Doughty discusses regional associations in Lima. Fleuret shows how Sikhs in Los Angeles become incorporated into networks of other Sikhs. Hirabayashi's group discuss the development among Indian-American migrants of a pan-Indian consciousness.

Not all of those authors make explicit how they obtained their information. Fleuret is especially remiss in that regard. Most, however, combine participant observation with various means of quantifying data, such as collection of diaries, daily expense accounts, life histories, and the like, or through administration of questionnaires built up from the results of participant observation.

The studies by Graves and Barnett represent opposite extremes of methodology. Seeking to discredit the "culture of poverty" conception of the urban poor, Graves made an attitude/personality survey and an economic survey of Navajos in Denver, much as a social psychologist would do. In contrast, Barnett does a close institutional analysis of a caste in Madras, showing how demographic movement and economic change (rural-urban migration, commuting, and encroachment by a city upon a formerly agricultural community) are causing changes within the caste and in its relations with other population sets.

Using a kind of dramaturgical approach, as suggested by Frankenberg, but owing much to Goffman[31] (though Barnett cites neither), Barnett begins with an analysis of two brief incidents in Old Town of Madras City.[32] In the first, a man refuses to invite a prestigious fellow caste member to his daughter's wedding reception, but is coerced into changing his action by other caste members. In the second, a Brahman priest, guilty of a minor infraction of a minor ceremony, is publicly beaten by the owner of the house at which the infraction occurred. The process of "making sense" of those two simple events carries Barnett through a description of caste relations and

mechanisms of change that go far beyond the neighborhood and Madras City to include all of Tamilnada State. Finally, he is led to propose that, contra Mitchel, members of the caste, "cannot simply alternate between village and regional zones of reference," because each point of view requires a distinctive ethic. Further, he says,

The relevant units then are not really city and village taken as mutually exclusive, delimited entities. Encompassing the city proper is the caste's regional ethnic-like identity and this non-local identity can also affect village segmentation.

SOURCES OF MIGRANTS

One other study deals with migration, but not migrant adaptation. Segal surveys contributions that various rural ethnic groups in East Africa have made to rural-urban migration, and points out that percentages of migrants differ from group to group, providing further evidence of the inadequacy of economic theories of migration that assume evenly distributed, culturally homogeneous rural populations. This is a good example of demography pointing the way to ethnography.

OTHER SPATIALLY UNBOUNDED POPULATIONS

Although migrants from a particular village, region, or ethnic group may settle together, migrants usually are populations that are roughly identifiable spatially. We have

31. R. Frankenberg, "British Community Studies: Problems of Synthesis," in *The Social Anthropology of Complex Societies*, A.S.A. Monograph no. 4, ed. M. Banton (London: Tavistock Publications, 1966). Frankenberg himself cites E. Goffman, *The Presentation of Self in Everyday Life* (New York: Doubleday & Co., 1959); E. Goffman, *Encounters* (Indianapolis: Bobbs-Merrill Co., 1961). Several other of his works are relevant.

32. Barnett, "Urban Is as Urban Does," p. 153.

already mentioned Spradley's research on tramp subculture, and we will again in the final chapter. His article in this sample reports on the same research. Although Uzzell's research is focused on four localities in Lima, the sampled article does not deal with a spatially bound population set, but with what he considers to be a developing social unit, constituted mostly of migrants though not including all migrants. He suggests ways that this unit, which is in some respects like a class and in others like an ethnic group, has been affected by migration, and how its development has reciprocally affected rates of migration and migrant adaptation.

Loveland discusses the rural Rama Indians on the Miskito coast of Nicaragua. She explains certain developments among the Rama in terms of local urban developments, to which the Rama must respond. Both Loveland and Uzzell imply a systemic point of view and treat the phenomena they discuss in a historical or processual way, as opposed to Spradley's largely situational approach.

SPATIALLY BOUNDED POPULATIONS

The next five authors in our sample reported research primarily directed to specific geographical localities. The authors are Mochon, Pelto, Epstein, Whiteford, and Nagata.

Mochon writes about the development of a "working class" suburb, presumably in Midwestern United States. Without specifying research techniques, she purports to show how decisions by the community as a whole have, over the years, affected the community. Pelto's article is more an essay on big-budget research than a substantive report of findings. Though located in an artificially created town near Mexico City, his work should prove instructive to any anthropologist in a position to amass a multi-specialty team capable of large scale

research. Epstein's study of irregular settlements around the newly created capital of Brazil treats the entire city system, explaining why the settlements developed and the part their residents play in the city.

Two other researchers deal with localities within cities. Whiteford studied in what we would call an irregular settlement in Popayán, Colombia. His paper is largely a discussion of problems and methods of fieldwork. However, in the substantive portions, he discusses the locality as a community and also talks about the ways its residents relate to the larger urban center of which the settlement is a part. Nagata discusses sub-ethnic differences between a Malay enclave in each of two Malaysian cities. To account for the differences, she talks about historical factors in the two cities, suggesting that the sub-ethnic differences represent adaptation to two different sets of situations.

COMPARISON OF RURAL AND URBAN SUBCULTURES

We have grouped the next three articles on the basis of their concentrating on differences between rural and urban subcultures. Again, the grouping could have been different. Several of the authors writing about migrants obviously addressed the same question. Our grouping is based on emphasis. In a sense, all comparisons of rural and urban subcultures are dealing with concerns similar to Redfield's: whether or not there are universal differences between the cultures or subcultures of rural and urban populations.

Dorjahn reports on a study of marriage practices and attitudes toward aspects of marriage among two samples of Temne males in Sierra Leone. One sample consists of 47 literate residents of a small town (Magburaka; population between 6,000 and 7,000). The other sample consists of 23 nonliterate residents of villages within a twenty-mile radius of Magburaka. Beginning with a knowledge of normative and strategic Temne marriage practices in rural places, Dorjahn examines marriage histories from both samples and also asks members questions about their marriage plans and preferences. He finds that while most of the marriages of urban dwellers were traditional, there were numerous differences between samples in the strategic use of the available practices, including a reduction of the number of wives per man in the urban sample. We find this an interesting study, and one whose design raises questions that we shall discuss further in the next chapter.

Provencher compares patterns of face-to-face interaction in a Malay village with similar behavior in a Malay settlement in Kuala Lumpur, arguing that situational differences in the settings require more "traditional" forms in the urban setting than in the rural one.

Contrasting with those two close studies is one that is remarkable for its superficiality and the ethnocentrism of its theoretical underpinnings. R. W. Thompson addresses himself to rural-urban differences in something called "individual modernization." "Modernization" has had considerable play in some circles. As best we can tell, it is a euphemism for the process by which non-Western people accept certain aspects of Western culture. This, of course, can lead to unbiased studies of culture contact and acculturation. More frequently, however, certain cognitive elements purportedly found in some subcultures in Europe, North America, and Australia are declared good, modern, necessary-for-development, and so forth, and are sought in other populations. Such an exercise is Thompson's. He relies on opinion survey and "behavioral observations" of samples of three populations in Buganda. The three populations are called rural, intermediate, and urban. Thompson devises questions which supposedly show

"future time perspective," "delayed gratification," both of which are presumed to be modern. For example, one question is,

Which would you prefer, one egg today or three eggs tomorrow? Another is,

Which would you prefer, a round trip to Nairobi today or a round trip to Europe or the USA in five years?[33]

Obviously, both questions may measure a number of things other than the way one thinks about time and delayed gratification (if I fall out of an airplane today, receiving a parachute tomorrow won't help me much), and both may be unintelligible. Nevertheless, Thompson correlates the answers with various traits and finds that modern values are most frequently associated with education and listening to radios.

OTHER STUDIES

Of the four remaining studies in our sample, two report on urban fieldwork that falls outside our other classifications, one is a theoretical discussion of proper kinds of urban research for anthropologists, and the other, is a discussion of Latin American cities in general.

Press does a functional analysis of folk medicine in Seville. Micklin and his associates make a componential analysis of responses given when they asked residents of a Colombian city for synonyms of *"loco."* Nutini suggests a typology of Latin American cities based on historical/functional criteria. Finally, Plotnicov's discussion has already been mentioned and will be again in the next chapter. We feel that Plotnicov's article should be required reading for all anthropologists who study urban places.

33. Thompson, "Rural-Urban Differences," pp. 69-70.

CONCLUSIONS

As we admitted at the outset, we did not choose these papers in such a way as to represent with exact proportionality what anthropologists have been doing in cities recently. Our choices, however, illustrate the extreme variety of interests, theoretical orientations, and research techniques—a variety that would have been even more evident if we had space for more than cursory summaries. The disproportionate emphasis on rural-urban migrants (which would be evident in any sampling) we feel to be temporary, not only because other questions will demand investigation, but also because understanding the behavior of migrants requires more detailed study of other parts of the urban context. Most conspicuously lacking, despite several notable attempts, are detailed institutional analyses of the cultural systems of entire cities and towns, and of regions. This, too, may well reflect our present degree of development, rather than theoretical orientations. Further discussion of that and other issues will be taken up in the following chapter.

For Further Reading

Cornelius, W., and Trueblood, F. M., eds. *Latin American Urban Research,* vol. 4. Beverly Hills: Sage Publications, 1974. The latest from Latin America.

Foster, G. M., and Kemper, R. V., eds. *Anthropologists in Cities.* Boston: Little, Brown & Co., 1974. How-I-did-it stories.

Mangin, W., ed. *Peasants in Cities: Readings in the Anthropology of Urbanization.* Boston: Houghton Mifflin Co., 1970. Mixed bag of articles, including a number of useful reports on formerly rural people (not all of them peasants) in third-world cities. Fairly vapid introduction.

Bibliography

Leacock, E. B., ed. 1971. *The Culture of Poverty: A Critique.* New York: Simon & Schuster.

Leeds, A. 1967. "Some Problems in the Analysis of Class and the Social Order." *Social Structure, Stratification, and Mobility.* Washington D.C.: Pan American Union, General Secretariat of the Organization of American States.

Lewis, O. 1966. "The Culture of Poverty." *Scientific American* 215: 19-25.

Redfield, R. 1947. "The Folk Society." *American Journal of Sociology* 52:294.

7 | Suggestions for Urban Research

INTRODUCTION

Since much of this book so far has been argumentative, it is appropriate that we conclude by suggesting directions of anthropological research in urban places that we find promising. First, let us make what peace we can with survey research.

It is clear that in urban studies, as in rural studies, the researcher must find out whether or not information obtained from a limited number of informants is broadly applicable, or if not, why not. Given practical limitations of time and personnel, some kind of device is required for providing such checks. One device is the questionnaire. The primary problem with questionnaires is that of deciding what the answers mean. Of course, the same problem exists in long, informal interviews—or for that matter, in conversations between old friends. It is a matter of degree: *ceteris paribus*, the more fleeting and superficial the relationship between investigator and informant, the greater is the likelihood of misunderstanding.

Several steps may be taken to improve the usefulness of questionnaires. First, it is inconceivable to us that a survey of a population would be made without first having done a great deal of ethnographic fieldwork among them (except, of course, for preliminary censuses). That is the only way to gain some assurance that questions asked will make sense to respondents, and it is the only hope one has for understanding what the respondents mean when they give one answer or another. A standard procedure when the ethnographer begins asking questions about a particular topic is to ask local informants what kind of questions to ask, and gradually to improve on the questions by asking further questions about the responses. By that means, as well as by simply listening to people talk and observing them, the ethnographer gradually gets a feel for what is meaningful for the population he is studying. Only then is he ready to standardize some questions into a questionnaire. And even so, he still must refine his questionnaire by submitting it to the criticism of members of the population. That, of course, precludes the use of tests or questionnaires developed elsewhere, even for other subcultures in the same general locality.

Generally speaking, we would apply the same reasoning to the theoretical underpinnings of the questions asked. The notion of "future orientation" makes a good example. It is a fiction that has been created largely in North America and Europe, in which certain kinds of responses to certain kinds of questions are held by convention to indicate the respondents' attitudes toward delayed gratification. There are difficulties with the construct even as it applies to the population sets in which it was developed, but we are not interested in discussing those problems. Even assuming that the imputed significance of responses is valid in the original population sets, we see no necessary relationship between questions and answers in other population sets.

Just to translate the questions into locally meaningful terms as, for example, Thompson seems to have done in the article cited in the last chapter (i.e., by speaking of eggs instead of, say, dollars) is not enough, because there is no guarantee that the answers show the respondents' attitudes toward delayed gratification. If there is an abundance of eggs, delaying eating them has no significance. In fact, one might have to eat food on hand immediately to avoid spoilage. At the other extreme, if food is extremely scarce, delaying its consumption might incapacitate one so that he is unable to obtain more food later on. Similarly, regarding Thompson's question about going to Nairobi today or to the United States or Europe in five years, at a certain age one might not expect to live five years, or one's future plans might be such that a trip is feasible now but will not be in five years, or even— heaven forbid—one might prefer going to Nairobi to going to the United States or Europe at *any* time!

None of that is to imply that theories cannot be tested cross-culturally. Quite the contrary. What we are saying is that the theory itself, and not just the instrument, must be translated into locally meaningful terms—something that can be done only after ethnographic study.

We suggest that even ethnographically validated questions are dangerous when they seek opinions or when the respondents must choose among a limited set of answers. That, of course, depends on the use to be made of resultant data. If I ask people whether or not they approve of the President's handling of foreign policy, for example, I may legitimately report the results of the survey, but little else. I do not know the reasons people had for responding as they did. Nor do I know what they meant by the terms "approve" or "disapprove." If I ask respondents to indicate whether they strongly approve, slightly approve, slightly disapprove, strongly disapprove, or have no opinion, I learn absolutely nothing more outside the answers themselves than I would from the first question. We suggest, therefore, that survey questions be limited to reporting of events, dates, places, and so forth, with the understanding always that even such "factual" data must be interpreted, and therefore remain problematic.[1]

NETWORK ANALYSIS

Network analysis, which has been introduced in preceding chapters, has come to be fairly well entrenched in the anthropological tool kit over the past two decades. We single it out in this chapter because it seems useful and because it has been represented as a technique particularly well suited for the study of complex, urban societies, the implication being that traditional techniques for studying small rural societies —particularly description of kinship and other institutions—are inappropriate for large societies. We would counter that to the extent that traditional descriptions have left out accounts of behavior that was not analyzable through consideration of institutions and formal groups, they have been inadequate for studies of rural populations as well. That does not mean that we are as sanguine as some of the proponents of network analysis about the potential value of the technique.

1. A. V. Cicourel, "Fertility, Family Planning and the Social Organization of Family Life: Some Methodological Issues," *The Journal of Social Issues* 23(1967):57-81.

Most accounts of the development of network analysis place its formal origin with a publication by Barnes in 1954.[2] However, most writers, including Barnes, point out that as a metaphor for social structure, the notion has been around much longer.[3] And many writers continue to use the term metaphorically, without making explicit statements about the nature of the networks they speak of. As Barnes has pointed out in a recent article,

. . . there is no such thing as a theory of social networks; perhaps there never will be. The basic idea behind both the metaphorical and the analytic uses of social networks—that the configuration of cross-cutting interpersonal bonds is in some unspecified way causally connected with the actions of these persons and with the social institutions of their society—this remains a basic idea and nothing more.[4]

Most formal treatments of networks have consisted primarily of representation, diagrammatically or mathematically or both, of arrays of dyadic relationships. This is most frequently done with undirected graphs in the case of symmetrical relationships such as friendship, or with di-graphs where nonsymmetrical relationships are involved, and with matrices. Obviously, graphs become unfeasible when more than just a few individuals are considered. Matrices overcome this difficulty and also allow mathematical manipulation. The most ambitious project so far is that of Alvin Wolfe in which he develops a scheme for the structural comparison of networks.[5]

Any kind of treatment of networks with more than a few members practically requires the use of a computer, so bulky are the data. Barnes reminds us that with "the addition of each new member the number of potential links increases by . . . twice the previous number of members."[6] With twenty members there are 380 possible links; with 100 members, 9900 possible links. And,

this is not allowing for multiplex relationships between dyads. Clearly, the data-processing capabilities of computers must begin very early to outstrip the ability of the fieldworker to observe and record relationships.

Indeed, it is just as well that this is so, because there appears to us to be a diminishing return of analytical revelation to investment in detail of network data. In his study of a dispute between two workers in a zinc plant, Kapferer gives an extraordinarily extensive treatment of the network of relations among the twenty-three workers involved and their relations with outsiders.[7] Yet, as Barnes says, "Much of what he has to say about the dispute is simply good situational analysis and could have been achieved without appeal to the idea of a network."[8]

The literature on networks is confusing because there is no standardized terminology, and many writers have felt free to create as many neologisms as they liked. We like the terminology used by Wolfe because of its relative simplicity. A social network is, for him, any model in which actors are linked in social situations. Any part of that

2. J. A. Barnes, "Class and Committees in a Norwegian Island Parish," *Human Relations* 7 (1954): 39-58.

3. The use of sociograms for descriptions of relationships of individuals in small groups is a limited kind of network analysis, the development of which predates the development of network analysis. However, it is virtually ignored in the anthropological literature, except by Barnes.

4. J. A. Barnes, *Social Networks*, Addison-Wesley Modular Publications 26(1972):2.

5. A. W. Wolfe, "On Structural Comparison of Networks," *Canadian Review of Sociology and Anthropology* 7(1970):226-44.

6. Barnes, *Social Networks*, p. 7.

7. B. Kapferer, "Norms and the Manipulation of Relationships in a Work Context," in *Social Networks in Urban Situations*, ed. J. C. Mitchell (Manchester: Manchester University Press, 1971).

8. Barnes, *Social Networks*, p. 13.

network he calls a set. He then defines five kinds of sets:

personal set—limited to the links of one person
categorical set—limited to links involving a type of person
action set—limited to links purposefully created for a specific end
role system set—limited to links involved in an organized role system
field set—limited to links (relationships) of a certain kind.[9]

Other characteristics, though, remain to be specified. For example, if we focus on relationships of a single person, does the set include links between those with whom he has links or not? Also, are we to include only direct relationships or also indirect relationships (i.e., where A does not know C, but knows B who does know C)? If indirect relationships are included, how many intervening links are to be allowed? Terms for some of these have been introduced, but we see no need at present to repeat them and thereby needlessly contribute to the confusion.

The difficulty of gathering network data should not necessarily be considered a fatal defect. If, by some magic, we could find out all the relationships of all the people in a large population and feed them into a computer, we presumably could generate a very detailed description of their society. But by the time we made the description, the structure would have changed. Moreover, we feel that what should be of major interest to anthropologists should not be static structures but the ways in which individuals and groups manipulate the parts of the structures that affect them, or in Aronson's words,

. . . we want to know *how* [action sets] . . . are selected from extended networks, that is, how "assets" or "resources" or "social capital" are converted to use in particular situations. What are the relative values of assets he has, and what restrictions are placed on their conversion? Why, more specifically, are some ties more potent than others? . . . [Action sets] in this sense are clearly the result or embodiment of purposive strategies and choice making (in allocating time, cultivating linkages, cementing alliances, proffering deference, and so on) which are the key assumptions in Barth's optative theory of society.[10]

It is with such questions in mind that Whitten analyzed the ways in which members of two populations, one in Nova Scotia and one on the northwest coast of Ecuador, manipulated what he calls their social capital. Particularly interesting is the fact that while Whitten elicited network information, he also paid attention to how he, as a member of the networks, was manipulated. What he found was a distinctive type of strategic use of networks in each of the two localities, which he was able to relate to the ecological (actually economic) niches of each.[11]

Although we can see possible value in the formal analysis of networks, we feel that the eventual yield of insights simply from the use of the metaphor may prove to be greater. Manipulations of network data are at a very low level of abstraction.[12] Thus it should come as no surprise that nontrivial

9. Wolfe, *Structural Comparison of Networks*, p. 229.

10. D. Aronson, "Social Networks: Towards Structure or Process?" *Canadian Review of Sociology and Anthropology* 7(1970):262.

11. N. E. Whitten, Jr., *Class, Kinship and Power in an Ecuadorian Town: The Negroes of San Lorenzo* (Stanford: Stanford University Press, 1965); N. E. Whitten, Jr., "Network Analysis in Ecuador and Nova Scotia: Some Critical Remarks," *Canadian Review of Sociology and Anthropology* 7(1970):269-80.

12. But not as low as some practitioners, who speak as though the networks existed independently of the analyst, appear to believe.

formulations arising from the data must depend on concepts outside of the data themselves, as was the case in Kapferer's study. On the other hand, limiting oneself to the metaphorical use of the concept can free the ethnographer from gathering extremely detailed network information and allow him or her to spend time looking for other kinds of data. In a study of the adaptation of migrants in four squatter settlements in Lima, for example, Uzzell surveyed a large number of householders, asking for the names, addresses, and employment of certain kinds of kin and fictive kin (eliciting thereby categorical personal sets). Then he asked who, if anyone, had provided assistance, such as helping the respondent find past and present jobs and housing. Responses included all manner of relationships. With those data and information about each respondent's present economic situation, Uzzell was able to infer some of the strategic uses people in the sample had made of what Whitten would call their social capital and the economic outcomes of different choices and of different resource bases.[13]

In summary, we feel that network analysis is an indispensable ethnographic tool, but that its use in theory construction probably is limited. We agree with Aronson that the real value of information about social networks lies in the inferences one may make from it about the optative processes at work in a culture or subculture, and not in revelations from it of putatively static social structures. Also, network analysis can be a means of describing relationships between different segments of an urban population; thus combining micro and macro perspectives in one mode of description.

MIGRATION STUDIES

The fact that a great number of anthropologists have studied some aspect of migration does not necessarily indicate that no more studies are needed, although demographic changes no doubt will soon call for different kinds of studies. We have two major complaints about most existing studies. First, considering the magnitude of migration to cities, particularly in the so-called third world, during the past thirty years, it is astounding that very few people have addressed the question of how the decision to migrate fits into the migrant's overall life strategies.[14] There have been surveys in the cities in which migrants were asked why they left home, but these have tended to be unenlightening. Conspicuously absent have been inquiries into why those who remained at home did *not* migrate. In short, there have been very few situational analyses of the optative context leading to migration.

Second, we feel that enough evidence is available now for anthropologists to reconceptualize migration. (In fact, accomplishing that probably would remove our first complaint.) In the literature, one reads about rural-urban migration, rural-rural migration, urban-urban migration, temporary migration, return migration, and the like. The image in all of this, whether intentional or not, is of two discrete cultural entities, like train depots. If one has, as it were, a round-trip ticket, the migration is temporary. If he or she travels one way, but decides later to return, it is return migration, and so on. The depots, the poles of the migration image, presumably remain the same; or we speak of changes in one or the other— usually in the city. Even Mitchell's treatment of the cultural activities of migrating tribesmen in Africa, who he says become essentially bicultural, still uses the train depot view of the origins and destination of migrants.

13. J. D. Uzzell, *Bound for Places I'm not Known to: Adaptation of Migrants and Residence in Four Irregular Settlements in Lima, Peru,* Ph.D. dissertation, University of Texas at Austin, 1972.

14. The study by the Salisburys in chapter 6 is an outstanding exception.

Such an image is, we feel, confusing at best, and at worst, misleading. There are indications that in many rural populations, formerly depicted as static and isolated, considerable migration has been going on for some time. As Peter Tobias remarked after a year in Grenada, "How do you use a polar model of migration when 50 percent of the adult males in your village are absent all the time—and spread all over the world"?[15] Also, it is often true that the array of options available to a village population are not only extremely variable but also multi-local, and the resultant variety of movements of people about a region, or even larger geographic area, makes a poor fit with our standard notions of migration. We think that if most of the studies of migration undertaken so far were regional in scope, we would not speak of migration at all, but simply of various life careers—a point of view that we feel would be more enlightening than the present one. It might, then, make sense to reserve the term migration for simultaneous movements of populations. At the very least, we feel that all the terms for "types" of migration should be dropped, not endlessly expanded.

HOLISTIC DESCRIPTION

We now return to one of the most formidable problems facing all social scientists, that of encompassing entire social or other cultural systems in one's analytical models. That problem has been treated variously: by retreating into statistical description, by dealing only with very large general variables, as in economics, or by maintaining the fiction, as many ethnographers have, that the small units they study intensively are culturally autonomous. Anthropologists feel the problem perhaps most acutely because of the paradox that both holism and ethnography are basic anthropological goals. How can we relate details of life in many small localities and in small populations to the structure of the large social system of which they are part?

SOCIAL STRUCTURE

We are in the habit of speaking of social structures of nations, regions, cities, tribes, or bands. We have several fairly standard ways of describing the social structure of tribes and some bands of hunters and gatherers whose membership can be defined fairly easily and which are organized primarily on the basis of kinship. However, when we come to states—or even to hunting and gathering bands that do not organize themselves by lineages—we fall into a quandary. States, by definition, are stratified; and most states are segmentally divided, as well. Most of the literature treats the strata as "classes." Yet as was shown in chapter 6, we find existing notions of class unsatisfactory.

Ethnic groups may divide society both horizontally and vertically. Ethnic groups are a special kind of population set that share a subculture. Although definitions vary, we follow Fredrik Barth, who feels that self-ascription and ascription by others is the distinguishing feature of ethnic groups. Barth says,

A categorical ascription is an ethnic ascription when it classifies a person in terms of his basic, most general identity, presumptively determined by his origin and background. To the extent that actors use ethnic identities to categorize themselves and others for purposes of interaction, they form ethnic groups in this organizational sense.[16]

15. Personal communication.
16. Fredrik Barth, "Introduction," in *Ethnic Groups and Boundaries*, ed., Fredrik Barth (Boston: Little, Brown & Co., 1969), pp. 13-14.

Barth's treatment of ethnic groups, particularly his emphasis on transactions between groups, we find most valuable. However, the structural characteristics of no society are exhausted by a description of ethnic groups alone.

We have spoken repeatedly of population sets with subcultures. As a subtype of such sets, ethnic groups are the most easily identifiable. Unfortunately, there is little agreement as to how to define—or identify—subcultures in general.

In other words, the very units of social structure are problematic. We shall return to this question in a moment. But first, a word must be said about the kind of analytical myth that should be used when we describe the social systems of a locality or region.

PROCESS AND OPTION

Beginning about three decades ago, some anthropologists began to criticize the fact that descriptions of social structure tended to portray static arrays of units with fixed interrelationships. When systemic descriptions were used, the systems tended to be closed, with homeostatic properties. Critics of that mythical orientation argued that, in fact, social and other cultural systems are better characterized as open and with constant change of relationships among elements and within elements.

More recently, a related kind of criticism has been heard, most notably from Barth and his followers, but very quickly from others, including sociologists such as Clyde Mitchell. Essentially, that criticism is that cultural systems have been described without reference to the choices and constraints on choices of actions by individuals and groups.[17] That point of view fits into the processual orientation (or grew out of it) because choices are seen as the motive force of processual social structure.

SOCIAL ORGANIZATION AND SOCIAL AND CULTURAL SYSTEMS

Elman Service, following Walter Goldschmidt, has distinguished between "social structure" and "social organization" by saying that the former should be used to refer to the configuration of groups in a society and the latter should refer to what Service calls "the network of statuses" and their accompanying roles, as well as the social structure.[18] "Status" in that usage is the actor's position in a social system. His or her "role" is the potential for behavior connected with that status. That is, the set of actions that people who recognize his or her status expect from him/her as a result of that status. Obviously a single status can imply different behavior potential for people with various statuses of their own. A general does not expect the same kind of behavior from a lieutenant that a private expects from him. At the same time, any given actor has a number of assigned statuses, depending on situations. And he or she may well be free to define situations in such a way as to utilize the most beneficial status. That is part of one's optative array.

In situations where one's status is not known beforehand to others in the interaction, one may be able to present himself or herself in such a way as to have this or that status attributed that otherwise might not be. Also, where one is unknown, he or

17. When we say that people *choose* among options, we do not mean to imply that this or that "rational" process is employed, simply that, in a given situation, certain actions are perceived as possible by the actor and that he or she—or it, in the case of a group—somehow arrives at performing one action instead of the others that were perceived as possible. The notion of rationality is culturally determined and it would be inappropriate to apply one culture's definition in the construction of our myth.

18. Elman R. Service, *Primitive Social Organization: An Evolutionary Perspective* (New York: Random House, 1962), p. 19.

she may be able to escape sanctions for not performing roles in expected ways. (This may, indeed, be the single most significant difference between society in small populations and society in large populations.)

Those considerations indicate that what Service calls social organization may be an extremely fluid and complex entity. Because in everyday usage "organization" seems to connote a stable set of relationships, we feel that it is better to speak of social *systems* rather than structures or organizations. Where the system includes more than interactions of members, we should speak of cultural system elements and relationships.

The simplest definition of system consists of two parts: A system has more than one element, and the elements are related to each other in specific ways. A *closed* system is one in which the only possible interactions of elements are those made possible by the original elements and relations, including their possible permutations. An *open* system is one in which new elements and new relationships may be introduced from the outside. By treating cultural systems as open systems, we may escape criticisms leveled at anthropologists who used the systems myth early in this century.

Elements of systems may themselves be systems. We may speak of a cultural system in which one element is the economy. That element itself may then be thought of as a system, its elements including, perhaps, various industries, capital, and distribution. Each of these elements may in turn be a system, and so on, until at the most basic level we arrive at a system whose elements are the economic transactions of single individuals. It was with that image in mind that we asserted earlier that network analysis is at a very low level of abstraction.

Crosscutting such a hierarchy of systems may be other kinds of subsystems. That is, elements at any given level may share elements at the next lower level.

Given the present state of the art of doing social science, *formal* description of cultural systems must be crude and rare. Nevertheless, we feel that it is useful to set as our goal such formalization, and to proceed as if it were possible or would become possible in the future. Throughout, of course, we should remain aware of the "as if" quality of this etic formalization, testing it against the emic formalizations of other peoples.

ELEMENTS OF CULTURAL SYSTEMS

We return now to the problem of deciding what should be our units of analysis. Without reopening the whole question of what "class" means, we should like to take advantage of our discussion of systems to add an additional objection to the Warnerian model: that it does not lend itself to systemic analysis. Most treatments of class in the United States and Western Europe consist of correlations of this or that trait with income and occupation. One is seldom treated to analyses of the systemic relations among classes. People in a given class are held to have certain characteristics, but one does not learn why. We attribute that, at least in part to our Calvinist heritage, which has been transmuted into psychological explanation of economic position. Nowhere is that more evident than in the culture-of-poverty formulation, which asserts that poor people are poor because they think and act like poor people because they are poor. Ideological objections aside, such formulations are just not very edifying. Marxist and neo-Marxist models are systemic in nature, but they are Western cosmologies, mirror images of Western capitalistic cosmologies, that are often hard to reconcile cross-culturally with empirical data.[19]

19. We do not, in our criticism of Marxian notions of class, mean to throw out the baby with the bath water. We feel that Marxist analyses of relations of urban center to the rural hinterland, as

We recommend, then, that the word "class" be returned to folk usage (*class* never having strayed far from that, in the United States anyway) and that it be employed only when one is describing Western European folk models of society or when it is coincidentally useful for analysis. If it should be necessary to speak of hierarchical rankings of a population, "levels" or "strata" will serve nicely, and without the connotative baggage.

POPULATION SETS

All population groupings may be labeled by the general term "sets." Sets may be identified by their relations with other sets as well as by characteristics of their members. Because it is possible (indeed, likely) for one actor to be a member of a number of sets which may or may not coincide with each other, we caution that criteria defining a set must always be made explicit. With that restriction, we maintain that any population set is a valid unit of analysis if it proves analytically useful.

GROUPS AND AGGREGATES

Two general types of population sets may be distinguished on the basis of the relations of their members to each other. These types are "groups" and "aggregates." We reserve the term "group" for those population sets whose members ascribe membership to themselves and other members, for whom gaining membership or losing it entails some mutually recognized behavior, and who stand in an exclusive set of relations to each other. (Barth's definition of "ethnic group," which we noted above, would follow from our more general definition.) All other population sets are aggregates. This allows us to clean up two other terms which are obscurely used in the literature. When the population of a *locality* also is a *group,* then we speak of a community. We do not find it useful to speak of communities except in spatial terms. Thus, whether or not the population of a locality is a community is an empirical problem.

UNITS OF ETHNOGRAPHIC DESCRIPTION

In urban studies, as in rural studies, the ethnographer must define a population set that is of a size that he or she can study, using standard ethnographic techniques. This might be an ethnic group, a local elite, the population of a locality, a bowling team, or whatever. Yet we add another ideal requirement: that the ethnographer seek to discover not only the culture of the population set on which he or she is focusing, but also the nature of relations between that set and any other sets with which it or its members interact significantly. Failing to do that, anthropologists working in cities (or elsewhere) must either degenerate into abstracted empiricism or remain in the condition of the blind men who studied the elephant. That is, the possibility of holistic ethnographic studies of large and complex systems depends largely on our success at focusing on the nature of relationships among different sets of population in such systems.

URBAN ETHNOLOGY

We distinguish between ethnography and ethnology on the basis of data source. Ethnology takes ethnography at its source of

---

developed by Baran and Frank, are useful. Brian Roberts has made a brilliant analysis of a region in Peru, using that model. P. A. Baran, *The Political Economy of Growth* (New York: Monthly Review Press, 1957); A. G. Frank, *Capitalism and Underdevelopment in Latin America* (New York: Monthly Review Press, 1967); B. R. Roberts, "The Provincial Urban System and the Process of Dependency," paper prepared for the seminar of New Directions of Urban Research, Institute of Latin American Studies, University of Texas at Austin, May 16-18, 1974.

data. When we speak of urban ethnology, then, we imply analysis of a number of ethnographies in a given urban place or region. Or we may also mean analysis that compares or integrates studies of a number of urban places or regions. It is here that cultural systems reach higher levels of analysis.

Implied in urban ethnology is an analysis of how population sets interact and how these ways of interacting constrain the optative universes of members. Within a given cultural system, it seems to us desirable to decide upon a single perspective to guide choices of data sets by ethnographers. One such choice might be conflict resolution among sets. For example in cities in the United States, courts provide a point of articulation between a variety of population sets, as do quasi-judicial activities of organizations such as neighborhood associations. We have suggested to students, although this plan has not yet been carried out, that an examination of such conflict-resolving institutions might well lead us to meaningful selection of population sets for ethnographic study, and that the resultant ethnographies would then provide further data on nonconflict relations among sets.

Of course, population sets are articulated with each other by individual members, either by overlapping memberships or by individual transactions. Eric Wolf has suggested that the anthropologists study those "brokers" who are marginal to sets, but who stand in the interstices between sets.[20] This is certainly a useful formulation. However, it is apparent that many population sets are articulated otherwise than by the kind of brokerage that Wolf describes—often as not, cumulatively, through a number of small transactions by members across set boundaries. Such transactions often occur in occupational and more public settings. Important tasks of the ethnographer of such settings are to study the interface of interaction systems that fit together although they have different cognitive bases, and to study the specializations of interaction systems in those settings. We might add that a valuable activity would be to locate and study the sites of various kinds of transactions, such as stores, offices, bars, restaurants, banks, transportation facilities, and other public places. The absence of members of a particular population set from such a site could be as informative as its presence.

Richard Adams has gone as far as anyone in attempting to describe a limited number of types of population sets in terms of their internal organization and their relations with other elements in a system.[21] Adams' theme is power relationships, but "power" is defined extremely broadly as control over the environment, one's environment including the environments of others. In one test of the predictive ability of Adams' model, sets of workers in northern Argentina described by Scott Whiteford were matched with some of the types theoretically proposed by Adams.[22] The fit in that trial seemed quite good, and we feel that Adams' model deserves serious attention.

Several urbanists have suggested the development of typologies of cities, much like the functional types devised by urban geographers, but with the goal of finding regularities between city types and cultural phenomena.[23] Interesting as such exercises

20. E. R. Wolf, "Aspects of Group Relations in a Complex Society: Mexico," *American Anthropologist* 58(1956):1065-78.

21. R. N. Adams, "El Poder: Sus Condiciones, Evolucion y Estrategia," *Estudios Sociales Centroamericano* 4(1973):64-141.

22. S. Whiteford and R. N. Adams, "Migration, Ethnicity and Adaptation: Bolivian Migrant Workers in Northwest Argentina," in *Migration and Ethnicity: Implications for Urban Policy and Development,* ed. H. Safa and B. M. Dutoit (The Hague: Mouton Publishers, 1974).

23. *See* for example, J. R. Rollwagen, "A Comparative Framework for the Investigation of the City-as-Context: A Discussion of the Mexican Case," *Urban Anthropology* 1(1972):51-67.

might be, we are frankly skeptical of their utility until systemic descriptions of urban places and regions are available.

DATA SOURCES OTHER THAN ETHNOGRAPHIES

If studies in and of urban places present special problems, they also provide special opportunities. The presence of formal institutions—commercial, industrial, judicial, and others—with records of past transactions, and the availability of census data and studies by members of other disciplines, imply a wealth of information often not available in more remote rural places, particularly among populations without a long tradition of writing. Media of mass communications and transportation provide their own sources of information, both explicit and implicit. All of these and many more rich sources of information stand waiting to be exploited by the ethnographer or ethnologist seeking additional perspectives for what he or she has learned through ethnography. And indeed an interesting study in itself would be of the types of information available and of its differential availability to, and use by, various population sets.

THE TRAGEDY OF REINVENTING SOCIOLOGY

Space has permitted only a partial and generalized suggestion of the kinds of studies we think should be made in urban places. It has been said that if urban anthropologists continue as they have been going, they will reinvent sociology—fifty years late. If by sociology is meant the kind of abstracted empiricism of which Mills complained, then that prediction is a gloomy one indeed and we should pack up and leave before doing the world that disservice. And such a development would be doubly tragic because it is avoidable—if we can resist the pressures to mass produce our studies, manufacture meaningless data for the sake of a spurious "hardness," and ape the analytical models of classical physics. The techniques are available. Intimacy and empathy are long overdue in urban studies. These we offer as social scientists who are also humanists. But as anthropologists we offer a difference that is more. As Leonard Plotnicov has remarked:

The difference between anthropology and other social sciences is like a difference in cultures. What makes us different is not *who* we study, but a cognitive framework that underlies the qualitative difference in *how* we look at things and *what* we see.[24]

For Further Reading

Canadian Review of Sociology and Anthropology vol. 7 (1970). Whole issue on networks.

Liebow, E. *Tally's Corner.* Boston: Little, Brown & Co., 1967.

Ogbu, J. U. *The Next Generation.* New York: Academic Press, 1974.

Spradley, J. P. *You Owe Yourself a Drunk.* Boston: Little, Brown & Co., 1970. Liebow's, Ogbu's, and Spradley's works are examples of what ought to be happening.

Bibliography

Barnes, J. A. 1972. *Social Networks.* Addison-Wesley Modular Publications 26:2.

Barth, Fredrik, ed. 1969. *Ethnic Groups and Boundaries.* Boston: Little, Brown & Co.

Bertalanffy, L. von. 1968. *General Systems Theory: Foundations, Development, Applications.* New York: George Braziller.

Mitchell, J. C., ed. 1969. *Social Networks in Urban Situations: Analyses of Personal Relationships in Central African Towns.* Manchester: Manchester University Press.

24. L. Plotnicov, "Anthropological Fieldwork in Modern and Local Urban Context," *Urban Anthropology* 2(2)(1973):251.

Glossary

Adaptation—In social science, changes in the individual (or population) that enable it to survive in, and better exploit, its ecological situation. This phenomenon corresponds to the concept of *plasticity* in biology.

Anomie—A state of social void or psychological confusion about the proper way of doing things, or a distorted relationship between goals and means of achieving them.

Band—*(See tribe, chiefdom, state.)* The simplest level of social organization, consisting of small populations (usually under fifty) with little role differentiation and no permanent leadership.

Central Place Theory—The assumption that in a territory uniformly endowed with population, resources, and means of communication, major settlements will develop in a standard pattern and be surrounded by lesser settlements of a standard relative size.

Chiefdom—*(See band, tribe, state.)* Societies with a few specialists who do not produce their own food, with established leaders, and with power concentrated in one person.

Class—A social unit or category in a system of stratification. "Social stratum" is probably a better term because it does not bear the connotation of income and occupation that is attached to the concept of class, particularly in the United States.

Community Study—Intensive study of a locality or social group within a larger society rather than extensive superficial study of the larger society.

Culture—A concept about learned, patterned, and shared behavior. A particular culture is the learned, patterned, and shared behavior of a particular population.

Cultural Relativity—An assumption by anthropologists that each culture has its own logic and that the behavior of participants in that culture must be viewed in terms of that logic rather than the logic of another culture.

Econiche—That segment of an ecological system that directly affects one kind of organism.

Epistemology—Basic assumptions about knowledge. Answers to the question, "How do we know ———?"

Ethnic Identity—A classification of a person in terms of his origins and cultural background.

Ethnocentrism—Has several meanings. It may refer to having a low opinion of another ethnic group, to having a high opinion of one's own ethnic group, or to the inability to understand the particular logical perspectives of another ethnic group.

Ethnography—Systematic description of cultures and societies from the perspectives of participants.

Ethnohistory—Culture history from an anthropological perspective.

Ethnology—Study of ethnographic data.

Folk-Urban Continuum—A contrast between rural and urban ways of life that is at the same time a contrast between simple and sophisticated, isolated and cosmopolitan, personal and impersonal, moral and amoral, and traditional and modern forms of community.

Food-Producing Revolution—A change in subsistence economies brought about by the domestication of plants and animals. Not revolutionary in the sense of rapid change, but in the sense of thorough change. This process of change occurred at different times in different places.

Gemeinschaft—A type of society in which relations are mostly personal and traditional.

Gesellschaft—A type of society in which relations are mostly impersonal and regulated by contract rather than status.

Group—A population whose members ascribe membership to themselves and other members, for whom gaining membership or losing it entails some mutually recognized behavior, and who stand in an exclusive set of relations to each other.

Holism—Description of an entire sociocultural system.

Human Ecology—The mapping of distributions of economic functions, ethnic groups, social pathologies, and other traits.

Linear Models—Models which assume a chain of causes, so that A causes B, which causes C, and so on.

Metropolis—A city that is so large and complex that it has and requires multiple centers.

Network Analysis—The analysis of social ties.

Normative—Conforming to standards of a social group.

Over-urbanization — Rapid urbanization without sufficient economic growth to support it.

Participant Observation—The method of study widely used by anthropologists. It involves the anthropologist in the community, and requires him to live there while studying it.

Peasantry—Poor and powerless food producers in complex large-scale societies.

Primary Relationship—A direct social relationship in which two people play several roles vis-à-vis each other.

Role—The behavior expected of an individual in a particular status.

Role Density—A measure of the average number of links in a social network, where links are pairs of roles between two people.

Scale—A measure of social magnitude which includes size, density, total and per capita production, energy consumption rates, and efficiency of information management.

Secondary Relationships—An indirect or very superficial social relationship in which the participants play only a single role vis-à-vis each other.

Situational Analysis—Social analysis that takes into account the effect of demographic and social contexts on norms, values, and behavior.

Slash-and-Burn Horticulture—A kind of food production in which fields are cleared by felling trees and brush, and by burning. The fields are periodically abandoned and new fields claimed from the forest.

Social Organization—The network of statuses and their accompanying roles, as well as the social structure.

Social Pathology—Behavior that is labelled as "sick" by the definers of deviance in society.

Social Structure—The configuration of groups in a society.

State—*(See band, tribe, chiefdom.)* A society with a structure of leadership and administration which is specialized into bureaucracies, and has at least three social strata.

Subculture—A subvariety of a culture. sometimes referred to as a *life-style*.

System—Has more than one element, and the elements are related to each other in specific ways. A *closed system* is one in which the only possible interactions of elements are those made possible by the original elements and relations, including their possible permutations. An *open system* is one in which new elements and new relationships may be introduced from the outside.

Tribe—*(See band, chiefdom,* and *state.)* A level of sociocultural integration that is less complex than the chiefdom level but more complex than the band level.

Urbanism—A kind of social, economic, political, and cultural organization in which participants are related to each other through their links with central places. Urbanism also refers to organization in central places.

Urbanization—The process by which rural peoples and societies become urban. Urbanization also refers to migration and adaptation of rural populations to cities and often connotes modernization and Westernization.

Urban Revolution—The evolution of urbanism. Called revolutionary, not because it occurs rapidly but because it changes culture thoroughly.

Index

t